Beat the Bulge

Dr Russel Kirkby

MBChB DA

MFGP M Prax Med

BSc(Hons)(Pharmacology)

MSc Sports Med

Note for Librarians: A cataloguing record for this book is available from Library and Archives
Canada at www.collectionscanada.ca/amicus/index-e.html
ISBN 1-4120-6605-0

book 1

*Printed in Victoria, BC, Canada. Printed on paper with minimum 30% recycled fibre. Trafford's print shop
runs on "green energy" from solar, wind and other environmentally-friendly power sources.*

TRAFFORD
PUBLISHING™

Offices in Canada, USA, Ireland and UK
This book was published *on-demand* in cooperation with Trafford Publishing. On-demand
publishing is a unique process and service of making a book available for retail sale to the
public taking advantage of on-demand manufacturing and Internet marketing.
On-demand publishing includes promotions, retail sales, manufacturing, order fulfilment,
accounting and collecting royalties on behalf of the author.

Book sales for North America and international:
Trafford Publishing, 6E–2333 Government St.,
Victoria, BC v8t 4p4 CANADA
phone 250 383 6864 (toll-free 1 888 232 4444)
fax 250 383 6804; email to orders@trafford.com
Book sales in Europe:
Trafford Publishing (uk) Limited, 9 Park End Street, 2nd Floor
Oxford, UK ox1 1hh UNITED KINGDOM
phone 44 (0)1865 722 113 (local rate 0845 230 9601)
facsimile 44 (0)1865 722 868; info.uk@trafford.com
Order online at:
trafford.com/05-1516
10 9 8 7 6 5 4 3 2

Contents

This program is presented in 2 books.

The First book is divided into two sections:

The Second Book is the Honesty Book.

This contains:

The first section of the first book discusses and provides the theory behind the program.

The Instructions show you how to put the program into practice.

This book:

1. WINNING THE BATTLE of THE BULGE

Are you tired of losing the battle of the Bulge?
Are you tired of trying magic- guaranteed- quick fix- weight- loss- cures that repeatedly fail?

Are you serious about trying to lose weight?

You are?

Then you need the **BTB Program!**
BTB?
WHAT IS THIS? = The Beat the Bulge program.
Read on and find out!
Are you really serious about trying to lose weight?
If you are looking for that simple, instant magic, no effort cure, read no further because you are not serious about losing weight and you are not going to either!
  BUT
If you are seriously serious about this battle, join me and I will show you how to achieve success.
This program started as a joint venture between myself and a colleague, Roderick Kerr, as it was our discussions years ago that stimulated the production of this program.

We, Roderick Kerr and Russell Kirkby, are Family Physicians with over 50 years of General Practice between us. We have been there, done it and have the T-shirt to show for it.
We are ordinary folk and work with ordinary folk in their day to day lives. We are at the coalface as you are. We have seen our patients battle manfully (and ladyfully) against the bulge. We have shared the triumphs and agonised over the failures. We have seen all the fad diets, the magic pills, the guaranteed cures. We are also both fellow battlers so have tried a number of them as well.

Winning the Battle

We have ridden the unhappy roller coaster of success and failure and when we look around us we still see many, many people who try as they might, still lose this battle!
Our own personal battles and those that we have shared with our own real live patients in the real world drove us to look deeper into this difficult question and try to find a practical solution.

Did we go to the massive medical tomes and vast store of information on the Internet and having gleaned the pearls of wisdom, closeted ourselves in a secret laboratory to produce the Wonder Drug?

Swallow this miracle cure and tomorrow you will look like your favourite movie star!

No! - Ours is not that kind of solution!
We talked about a practical solution and both had similar ideas about what we should do. We planned to try and produce a practical program that was a program fashioned by the needs of everyday working people who have to fight the battle on their own turf with their own resources - not for them the health hydro, the personal trainer, the expensive designer drugs.

Unfortunately for me, Rod moved on to pastures new but the seed was sown and this program is the result– albeit a few years later. I would like to acknowledge his input in stimulating us to find a solution.

This program will work if you are seriously serious about losing weight and prepared to put in the effort required. Sounding too difficult already -think it means a life of deprivation and spartanhood?
Not a bit of it!
It does require commitment and application.

No, I do not guarantee "a body to die for doll!", nor the fountain of eternal youth.

What I do guarantee is that if you follow this program you will enjoy the benefits of a healthier lifestyle and achieve a healthy body size.

The program will provide the tools that make this possible and eventually second nature and easy!

The aim is to put both years on your life but more importantly *life* in those years.

AND

it will not cost you an arm and a leg

NOR

will you change back to a larger size once the program is completed.

Give your enthusiasm and commitment and that is all.

The program will give you the tools.

Solution?   Program?   Tools?   What are these?

Patience!   You will soon see.

Why should you be concerned if you are overweight?

First a Patient Scenario -an all too common one!

Mr Billy Bloop is 1.73 m tall and weighs 123 kg with most of the weight concentrated around his waistline.

He used to be a star athlete but since stopping sport at the age of 23 he progressively gained weight until now at 45 most of his clothes do not fit him and the ones he wears are ill-fitting and uncomfortable.

He is in a stressful job and has no time to exercise. He eats meals on the run and consumes a large amount of junk food.

One day he develops a pain in his belly and is feverish. He is ill and dehydrated.

The doctors struggle to put up a drip, as his veins are difficult to find in his chubby arms.

The doctor examining him has difficulty feeling his abdomen, as he has to feel through a few centimetres of blubber. He decides to do an abdominal X-ray. This has to be repeated, as the standard settings on the X-ray machine do not make the picture clear. Eventually an ultrasound is performed and the problem of an inflamed gallbladder is found. He requires surgery.

At the operation the surgeon mutters under his breath about the difficulties of operating on overweight people, as does the anaesthetist.

Both their jobs are made more difficult by the problems posed by the excess weight.

After the operation he has to spend some time in an intensive care unit as gallbladder surgery is close to the diaphragm and breathing is compromised. Because of the added load of his weight he has to remain on a ventilator for a day or two.

He develops a blood clot in his leg as well as pneumonia as complications. Both are potentially serious and prolong his hospital stay and add enormously to his medical bill.

Quite a story and tale of woe. Is this not a little farfetched?

Not really. If you really want to see if something is significant look to the insurance people. These folk take no real risk. If you are going to cost them money and influence their profit margins, your policy will be loaded.

Basically these people take a gamble on the odds or chances of you dying. They bet on your life and your chance of dying. If they get their figures wrong they will pay out too much and be down the tubes. The fact that some of the most successful companies are insurance companies should tell us something.

THIS IS WHAT HAPPENS TO OVERWEIGHT PEOPLE:

Actuaries have studied this and their figures show:

- an increased mortality of 5% even if you are only 10 to 25 lbs (5-10 kg) overweight

  This means that your chances of dying are 5% greater than someone of the same age with a normal weight.

  Actuaries have tables that predict the risk of death or disability with different conditions at any particular age.

- If you are 25-40 lbs. {10-20Kg} overweight, this results in up to a 31% greater chance of dying than someone of the same age but a normal weight.

- 45-60 lbs. {22-30Kg} overweight results in a 44%greater risk.

- 60-80 lbs.{30-40kg} overweight results in a 65% greater risk

- 80lbs or more (40Kg or more) results in a 123% greater chance of dying than someone with a "normal' weight and the same age.

OVERWEIGHT PEOPLE ARE:

- More difficult to examine
- More difficult to investigate
- More difficult to treat
- Often have a longer recovery period
- Have a greater chance of more complications.

Then there is prejudice and discrimination -no doubt about it.

(And the difficulty in finding clothes that fit!)

An overweight friend of mine told me that she did not like to consult a doctor about backache or pain in the knee because the first response was always:

"Well if you weren't so overweight...." or "Well, it's because of your weight."

Ever since I heard that I have been more conscious of my own innate bias and thoughts. When someone who is overweight presents with any complaint e.g. shortness of breath or pain in any musculoskeletal area it is hard not to involuntarily think: "Well what do you expect?"

For the best health care you need someone in there battling for you in the most positive frame of mind.

You don't need him or her to be thinking, even subconsciously: "If this person takes so little care of him or herself what do they expect?"

In the ideal world this should not happen.

But this is the real world and it does!

In the ideal world there would also not be anyone with a problem of weight control.

Thus unfortunately there are not many positive aspects to being overweight.

DO NOT DESPAIR -
This is not meant to send you into the depths of depression. We are here to help, precisely because this mindset prevails.

LOOK AT YOUR LIFE:
Answer the following questions:
Are you happy or sad?

What makes you happy?

How much *time* do you have for yourself each day?
What would happen if you were not here? I.e. died or ended up ill and incapacitated?

Would life stop or go on?

So why worry - BE HAPPY AND GET HEALTHY

THERE IS NO DOUBT THAT:
You are far more valuable alive and well than ill and decrepit or unable to function at full capacity.
You can do anything better or more efficiently if you are healthy, happy and in good shape and condition.

Hence there is no excuse for not investing in health.
If you don't have the *time* or do not want to put aside this *time* - then you are really not **serious** about **winning the battle of the bulge.**

If you don't have the time to invest in your health my advice is:

Take out the best insurance policy you can find because your family is going to need it. When all is considered, you are not investing in the only thing that really matters - if you do not have the best health you can muster for yourself, you have nothing at all.

If your house was burning down, you bet your life you would do everything in your power to get out of there and save your life.

If you would do that in an acute crisis situation, why will you not do it in the chronic situation?

What do I mean?

I am asking you to bet on your life.
Improve those odds the insurance actuaries make their profit on.

I will present the evidence if you require scientific proof but the way you can protect your quality of life is in **taking control of the situation yourself.**

How many people over the age of 100 do you know?

We are all destined to die and I am not offering immortality.

SO WHAT AM I OFFERING?
HERE IT IS:
THE BTB Program
The Beat the Bulge Program

This offers the best protection for Quality of Life i.e. Life in the years that are allotted to you.

How?

This program is designed to change your behaviour - That is the way you live your life.

It is a behaviour modification program and it also incorporates self hypnosis as an aid to adhering to the program.

Behaviour modification?

What is that? What about the Hypnosis lark?

Sounds like psychological mumbo jumbo and hard work.

Do not worry. Read on and you will soon see how to be healthy and happy.
All will be revealed!

It is not an instant swallow-this-pill-lie-back-and-be-cured or a new super-duper-major-discovery diet.

The fad diets don't work and neither do any instant pills or potions.

Why should they?

There is something perverse about Life.

Think about it.

11

I am pretty sure that nothing, or just about nothing that is of real value to you, has been acquired easily and with no effort.
That which is most valuable usually required a lot of hard work, commitment and dedication- but it was all worth it in the long run. Think of finishing school, perhaps qualifying at your chosen occupation, buying an apartment or a house.

We are asking you to change your behaviour and our program will show you how.
It is designed to progressively and incrementally introduce you to a new approach. It will require **effort, commitment and dedication** - all good basic sound qualities which you possess.

What works and will work for you **forever** is a change in the way you act and behave.

It is your actions or behaviour that have resulted in your being overweight. This has occurred over time and needs to be reversed. *Only if you change the behaviour or pattern of behaviour will you be permanently cured.*

In the days of yore our ancestors used to eat to live. When we were out hunting in prehistoric times we hunted and ate when we were hungry.
We also had to stay in pretty good shape to stay out of harm's way.

WHAT OF THE MODERN ERA?
We are bombarded with enticements and exhortations to indulge in a wide variety of tantalising foods and beverages. We are stimulated to eat, eat and eat. It is easy to   obtain - we don't have to hunt for it - it is there on a platter. We don't even have to stay in shape to run away from danger - we can just climb into a fancy vehicle and drive away.

Our behaviour has changed.
Instead of eating out of necessity, we now eat for pleasure.

And yes – it is fun to eat. It is sociable, pleasant and enjoyable. No doubt about it - but if we do not do so sensibly, we will pay the price.

Our aim for you is a healthy happy life.

That is really what you must decide.
Do it now and **decide whether you want to bet on your life** and **what bet you are going to lay.**

If you decide it is too hard and that you enjoy food too much and that you will wait for an easy solution (a pill, a diet, an operation), give up now.

There is not one, and there never will be one. If there was, there would not be any overweight people.

Decide to take your chances. Eat, drink and be merry and forget about tomorrow. Hopefully nothing will happen and you will have an uneventful and enjoyable life until one sudden final cataclysmic event ends your life with no pain or suffering.

That is if you are an inveterately optimistic gambler.

Whatever you do don't waste any further money on instant cures. Rather spend it on the good life and more food.

But if you want to hedge your bets and are more practical, you will know that in the developed world the acute and infective causes of death are less likely to get you than the chronic ones. Most of us will die from a cancerous process or a disease of the blood vessels.

I am not being morbid or depressing but stating the facts. The more medicine cures the "natural" causes of death, the more likely we will be to suffer the chronic causes.

You can be as good as you like, eat sensibly, don't smoke, do all the right things but the Grim Reaper is still "gonna get ya!"

So what can you do?

You can do the best you can to achieve the best quality of life before the scythe takes its final arc.

More than any drugs, lotions, potions or pills, **the behaviours** that will give you the best chance are **eating correctly and exercising**. Yes, you may need some pills, potions and the magic scalpel sometime and then you should be off to your local medico.

BUT .....

How best to aid and abet the other elements of health care and **what you can do for yourself** is to adopt the correct eating and exercise behaviours.

Here is how you do it:

THE BTB program

Kirkby's Beat the Bulge Program.

What is a behaviour modification program?
Sounds too much like psychological mumbo jumbo and science speak?
Well the reason why you are overweight is that you take in more energy than your body needs. The excess is stored as fat and there begins the problem.

Why do you eat too much?
Your eating pattern or behaviour is incorrect. It needs to be changed or modified.
Our goal is to modify your behaviour. We want you to eat correctly.
Why don't we just say so?
I am not sure but the main reason is probably that it sounds more impressive when you are giving a talk or writing a paper to talk about **behaviour modification** rather than "How to eat right!"
In essence however the principles of behaviour modification are applicable across the broad spectrum of human behaviours.

Why do we need a program?

Probably because we are human beings with all the failings and human frailties that this encompasses.

We know what is right. Why can't we say, "Stop eating that lovely ice-cream and eat all the healthy foods we know about and you won't have a problem!"

Of course we can and I am sure you have said this -probably many times.

The fact that you are reading this and looking at losing weight or beating the bulge is proof enough that simply saying so and knowing what to do is not good enough.

Most of us need to have a structure and guidelines to achieve our aims.

We can read and write and have careers.
How did we get there?
We were sent to school and learnt our lessons and passed exams.
Often we did not enjoy all of it and may not have thought a lot was

necessary. At the end of school we chose a course and did that as well. The same applies in that there were parts of the course that we enjoyed but also some we did not. However to achieve our goals we just had to do them.

We followed the *program and* this brought us success.

This program is no different.

There will be some grind but the end result will be success

If you stick to the program.

One added advantage is that this program, if followed, ensures success.

Contrast it with a keen young sprinter aiming at an Olympic gold or a world record. Try as he might and train as hard and as dedicatedly as he may, he may never achieve a sub 10 second 100 meter time if he does not have the genetic endowment or potential to do so. If the ligaments and muscles of his body are not superb and he does not have enough fast twitch fibres he is never going to get there. He may be good but he will never achieve his goal because it is impossible and not physiologically attainable.

But with this program your goal is eminently attainable.

You were born with a genetic potential to have a healthy build.

Somewhere along the way things have gotten out of hand and the slow slippery slide to poorer health has set in!

But you have the genetic potential. You just need to train to attain it. Training is nothing more than adaptation to increasing levels of stress or effort.

This program is your training schedule. We are giving you a structured program to follow.

Just as an athlete trains to improve fitness and skills and achieve excellence, so will you.

The path to excellence begins slowly and the training progressively intensifies.

Start low go slow.

Similarly for someone training for an athletic event when unfit, the first step is the hardest. -**To decide to do it.**

A good training program will build an athlete up slowly. Each step follows once the adjustment or adaptation has occurred. Eventually the training program becomes enjoyable and part of daily living.

The rewards of achievement make it easier and then the program is part of your life.

Start low, go slow- soon results will show!

Please note that the **training becomes more intense** *not* more difficult.

Think of dragging yourself out to pound the streets in an attempt to get fit. It is hardest at the beginning when your lungs cry out for air and your aching muscles demand a rest. Once you get fit it becomes so much easier and you are able to push harder with very little discomfort.

Getting through that initial patch is so much easier if you have a training schedule to follow. A successful training program has specific tasks with specific end points and goals.

It also makes it easier if you have a fellow sufferer or trainee to share the highs and lows.

<u>That is what we aim to do</u>
- You have the potential
- We have the program -the training schedule.
- Follow it and you will succeed!

For it to succeed we just need you to commit to it and follow it carefully.

Are you seriously serious?

If you are you can only win in this race- It is the race for **quality of life.**

What are we aiming at?

  - **A healthier and slimmer you.**

How does this program work?

This program **has a definite goal.**

Health is not merely the absence of disease.

HEALTH is a "State of physical, mental and spiritual well-being.

As Family Physicians we believe in **the whole person.**
We want you to be in a better physical and mental shape at the end of this program than when you started, and have a blueprint to continue improving for LIFE!

<u>GOAL:</u>
  To improve your health by instituting the BTB program

"But", you may well complain, "I want to lose weight!"
So you will, but the aim is not just to lose weight for weight's sake

and then regain it once the program is over.

In simple language:

Do what we say and you will look better, feel better, do better and be better!

At the end of the program you should find it easy and desirable to stick to your new healthy lifestyle.

Different people have different needs and different lifestyles so our program is structured to accommodate your individuality.

This book is basically a training program to lead you into a new healthy lifestyle.

It is not a fad diet that will get you slim, only to let you balloon back at the end of it.

We also do not advocate that you live on celery leaves or some exotic food that you would never eat in the normal life you live.

We aim to help you in your own environment and your own culture with the food you and the rest of your family are used to. We do not want to punish the rest of the family and make them eat dried toast and water. We aim to help you eat what they eat but in the correct portions and amounts.

Of course there are going to be times when you regress and we do not believe that it is then the "end of the world".

We have a plan for this, as any good program should be able to help you through adversity.

At the end of this program you should be trained to do the correct things automatically.

How will we do this?
- This is a program that lasts for 10 weeks.
- At the beginning and the end you will evaluate your health

The package consists of 2 books

    1. Beat the Bulge

        1.1 Why and What?

        1.2 Instructions - How? The tasks

    2. Honesty Book

1.1   Beat the Bulge. Why and What?

Here you can read the theory and the plans.

It will explain the whys and the wherefores and theory behind the tasks you are set.

In order to change your behaviour we will present facts to convince you of why you need to change. We will summarise these in the way we understand them. This is to gain a better understanding of the tasks you will be set.

And if you require even more documented scientifically referenced data - read a medical journal!

1.2   The Instructions - Tasks or Action Plans-How?

You will be set tasks to do each week. These appear in the **Instruction/ Action plans/Tasks section.**

This is a **summary** of all the **tasks** or **actions** you have been set.

This is the program structure without the theory behind it.

Each week you will be set a new task. The program is progressive in that each builds upon the previous week's work.

This is the **instruction manual -** Do what it says and you will lose weight and achieve improved health!

2. The Honesty Book

The lynchpin of the program is your Honesty Book.

In your Honesty Book you will have to record the results of your tasks.

Everyone following this program MUST fill in his or her Honesty Book.

This is crucial and the focus point of this program.

The Honesty Booklet is a daily diary that you keep on your person 24 hours around the clock. When in bed you may compromise by putting it on your bedside table!

This is to ensure you record every morsel that passes your lips into your mouth and also to record other factual information that will help with your training program.

How long does all of this take?

At the beginning and end of each week we need about **10 minutes** of undivided attention and enthusiasm. This period will be needed to understand the proposed program and to review it at the end of the week.

Each day will require a maximum of **15 minutes** - in divided segments to record in the Honesty book and collate at the end of the day.

Can you afford this time?

Can you afford not to spend this time on your health?

I am beginning to sound like a stuck record but I want you to really consider this thoughtfully. Without your health most other aspects in your life are diminished.

If you do not have this time, or rather are not willing to invest this time in your health, then you are not serious about this project and you do not really want to lose weight. Our program will not work for you and we don't think there is one for you.

BUT for those **seriously** serious types who are soon to be slimmer ……...

LET'S GO AND GET STARTED!

The plan now is to enter the program. Start it by performing the tasks.

Go to the task book and start at the beginning.
There is a little theory and some information in the Task book and the Honesty book but they are meant to be the practical part of the program.

What follows in the rest of this book is some more theory and some facts you may find helpful. These you can read now or at the appropriate stage in the program. For example when you come to the week where you make your hypnosis tape but you feel uneasy about this then go to the chapter in the Main book which tells you more of the theory behind it.

You can choose to read on or you can choose to go to the Instructions on page 93 and get started!

2.   **Health Status**

Perhaps we are genetically engineered to have a lifespan of 120 years.

I do not know any people of that age. In fact I do not know anyone above 100 years of age. In the developed world people are living longer. If you have access to good food, sanitation and medical care you are unlikely to die from the acute diseases such as pneumonia or diarrhea.

The things that will get you in the end are degenerative diseases, blood vessel diseases and the cancers.

In short the only recourses you have against these unpleasant facts are to eat well, exercise, keep your bodyweight down, have a low blood pressure, low cholesterol, low blood sugar and do the necessary screening for diseases at various ages. Your own doctor will discuss these with you and perhaps decide on some medication strategies such as aspirin where appropriate.

This program should have an effect upon your weight, your sugar, your cholesterol, your blood pressure and your exercise ability. All of these are necessary for a good quality life. This is why we emphasise the measurement of these parameters. Getting them into line can improve your health.

This is why we believe you need to assess your health before and after this program.

The aim is to make you healthier and measuring this will help to assess your health risk.

Your aims should be:
- Reduction of weight if you are overweight
- Maintenance of a healthy lifestyle
- Regular exercise
- A blood pressure of 120/80 mm Hg or lower if you are older than 18 years of age

- A fasting blood sugar below   6 mmol/l or 120 mg/dl

- A total Cholesterol of 5 mmol/l or 200mg/dl or lower
  5.17 mmol/l = 200mg/dl

- A HDL as high as possible preferably > 1.56 mmol/l
  HDL = your "healthy" cholesterol   > 60mg/dl

- A LDL below 3.0 mmol/l or 115 mg/dl and even better if
  Below 2.6 mmol/l or 100 mg/dl
  LDL = your "bad" cholesterol

These you need to discuss with your Doctor but achieving these will definitely afford you benefits in your health.

All men over 40 and women over 50 should *consider* taking a small dose of aspirin as a preventative measure against stroke and heart attacks. There are potential side effects as well as benefits so this should be discussed with your own doctor to assess your own benefits or otherwise.

3.   **The Food Pyramid**

The Food Pyramid *Recommended portions*

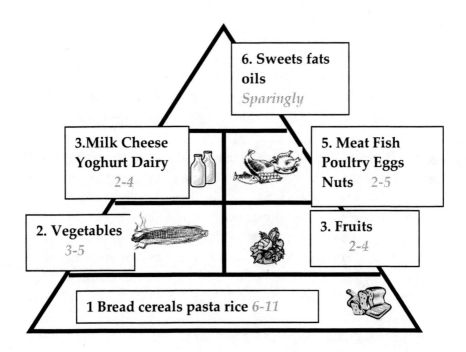

The figures in gray are the number of recommended portions one should eat per day. I.e. more from the base of the pyramid and less from the top.

The Food Pyramid, developed by the US Department of Agriculture, can help you choose from a variety of foods so that you eat the nutrients you need. The suggested serving sizes can help you control the amount of calories, fat, saturated fat, cholesterol, sugar or sodium in your diet.

Servings, portions and the use of these terms.

You will note here, there is mention made of *servings* as opposed to our mention of *portions*. These you will come across in the instructions section. We define a **portion** as the:

Area of the palm of your hand

A 240ml cup

Fruit the size of a tennis ball or two golf balls

Fats, sweets, oils = 1 tablespoon

Generally you can consider one serving to be equal to one portion although there are some differences e.g. below you will see one *serving* of group 1 is said to be 1/2 cup of rice, cooked cereal or pasta or1 cup of ready-to-eat cereal.

Now if you correlate with our portions as stated in our energy value of the different groups you will note that we have called one cup of 240ml a portion but graded the cereal as having a "low" energy value of 100 Kcals and the rice or pasta as having a "high" energy value of 200 Kilocalories. So in practical terms servings = portions. Servings is the term used by the US Dept of Agriculture and as they developed the concept of the Food Pyramid when referring to it servings is the term used.

Bread, grain, cereal and pasta form the base. Group 1

At the base of the food pyramid you will see the group that contains breads, grains, cereals and pastas. These foods provide complex carbohydrates, which are an important source of energy, especially for a low-fat meal plan. You can make many low-fat choices from foods in this group. You need 6 to 11 servings of these foods in a day. One serving of this group can be:

- 1 slice of bread
- 1/2 cup of rice, cooked cereal or pasta
- 1 cup of ready-to-eat cereal

Try to eat whole-grain breads, cereal and pasta for most of your servings from this group. Whole-grain foods (which are made with whole wheat flour) are less processed and retain more valuable vitamins, minerals and fiber than foods made with white flour.

Vegetables Group 2 and Fruits Group 3

Fruits and vegetables are rich in nutrients many are excellent sources of Vitamin A, vitamin C, folate or potassium. They are low in fat and sodium and high in fiber. The Food Pyramid suggests 3 to 5 servings of vegetables each day. One serving of vegetables can be:
- 1 cup of raw leafy vegetables
- 1/2 cup of other vegetables, cooked or raw
- 3/4 cup of vegetable juice.

The Food Pyramid suggests 2 to 4 servings of fruit each day. One serving of fruit can be:
- One medium apple, orange or banana
- 1/2 cup of chopped, cooked or canned fruit
- 3/4 cup of fruit juice

Count only 100% fruit juice as a fruit, and limit juice consumption. Many commercial bottled juices come in containers that hold more than 2 servings – which can add lots of sugar and calories to your daily diet. Punches, "ades " e.g. lemonade and most fruit "drinks" have only a bit of juice and lots of sugar.

Dairy Products Group 4

Products made with milk provide protein and vitamins and minerals, especially calcium. The Food Pyramid suggests 2 to 3 servings each day. If you are breastfeeding, pregnant, a teenager or a young adult aged 24 or under, try to have 3 servings. Most other people should have 2 servings daily. Interestingly, cottage cheese is lower in calories than most other cheeses - one cup counts as only 1/2 serving of milk. Go easy on high-fat cheese and ice cream. Choose non-fat milk and yogurt and cheeses made from skim milk because they are lowest in fat.

Beans, Eggs, Lean Meat and Fish Group 5

Meat, poultry and fish supply protein, iron and zinc. Non-meat foods such as dried peas and beans also provide many of these nutrients.

The Food Pyramid suggests 2 to 3 servings of cooked meat, fish or poultry. Each serving should be between 2 and 3 ounces. (60-90g.)

The following foods count as one ounce of meat (30g)

1 ounce =30g

- One egg
- 2 tablespoons of peanut butter
- 1/2 cup cooked dry beans
- 1/3 cup of nuts

Choose lean meat, fish and dry beans and peas often because these are the lowest in fat. Remove skin from poultry and trim away visible fat on meat. Avoid frying these foods. Moderation is the watchword when it comes to nuts because they are high in fat.

Fats and Sweets Group 6

A food pyramid's tip is the smallest part, so the fats and sweets in the top of the Food Pyramid should comprise the smallest percentage of your daily diet. The foods at the top of the food pyramid should be eaten sparingly because they provide calories but not much in the way of nutrition. These foods include salad dressings, oils, cream, butter, margarine, sugars, soft drinks, candies and sweet desserts.

Sugars found naturally in fruits and milk are not a problem. It's the added sugars that need to be limited because they provide calories but few vitamins and minerals. You'll find sugar-laden food at the top of The Food Pyramid. Added sugars can be found in soft drinks, candy, jams, jellies, syrups and table sugar we add to coffee and cereal. Added sugar can also appear in sweetened yogurt, soups, spaghetti, sauces, applesauce and other items where you wouldn't suspect it unless you check the list of ingredients.

Here are some guidelines for added sugar based on calories in the daily food choices:

Don't be worried about Calories and Kilojoules if you don't understand these at the present. All will become clear in Chapter 5.

- 1,600 calories (6,720 Kj) - Limit sugar to 6 teaspoons per day or 22 grams per day.
- 2,200 calories (9,240)Kj)- Limit sugar to 12 teaspoons per day or 44 grams per day.
- 2,800 calories (11,760 Kj)- Limit sugar to 18 teaspoons per day or 66 grams per day

Fat Intake.

Medical experts from the American Heart Association recommend that Americans limit dietary fat to 30 percent of daily calories. Here are the fat grams allowed based on daily calories:

The amount of fat you can eat is based on your caloric limit.
- 1,600 calories (6720 Kj) - Limit fat to 53 grams per day.
- 2,200 calories (9,240 Kj) - Limit fat to 73 grams per day.
- 2,800 calories (11,760 Kj) - Limit fat to 93 grams per day.

You don't need to count fat grams every day, but it's a good idea to do a "fat checkup" occasionally to be sure you're on the right track. Here's how to figure the number of grams of fat that provide 30% of calories in your diet:

Multiply your total day's calories by 0.30 to get your calories from fat per day. If you eat 2,200 calories, multiply 2,200 by 0.30. The

29

result is 660 calories from fat.

Divide calories from fat per day by 9 (each fat gram has 9 calories) to get your grams of fat per day. So in our example, divide 660 calories by 9 and you get 73 fat grams.

The following are some guidelines put out with the Food Pyramid. Part of the BTB program is to take you through a process to calculate the amount of energy intake you should aim at to stay at the same weight.
What follows are The American National Academy of Sciences Guidelines and are for information here as we are discussing the Food Pyramid in general.

Your own values will be worked out later so don't take these as guidelines to be rigidly followed.

You need to consume enough calories every day in order to ensure your body has the nutrients it needs. How many calories that actually amounts to depends on a variety of factors including your:

•   Age

•   Sex

•   Size

•   Activity level

•   Whether or not you are a pregnant or breastfeeding woman

•   Whether you have a chronic illness.

The Food Pyramid

The National Academy of Sciences recommends the following calorie categories:

- 1,600 calories (6,720 kilojoules)- Many sedentary women and some older adults

- 2,200 calories (9,240 Kilojoules) - Children, teenage girls, active women and many sedentary men.

- Women who are pregnant may need around 500 calories more per day and an additional 300 calories for breast-feeding.

- 2,800 calories (11,760 kilojoules) - Teenage boys, active men and very active women.

It is possible that you may fall between calorie categories on the chart. If you are then you will need to estimate servings. For example, some less active women may need only 2,000 calories to maintain a healthy weight. If you are at this calorie level, 8 servings from the grain group would be about right.

How Many Portions/Servings Are Right For You?
According to your food requirements or how many calories or Kilojoules you need to ingest, you can address the question of how many servings/portions of each food group you need. :

The following chart has some recommendations:

The Food Pyramid

Recommended number of servings of each group	Lower About	Moderate About	Higher About
Calories	1,600	2,200	2,800
Kilojoules	6,720	9,240	11,760
Grain Group servings (6-11)	6	9	11
Vegetable Group Servings (3-5)	3	4	5
Fruit Group servings (2-4)	2	3	4
Milk Group Servings (2-3)	2-3	2-3	2-3
Meat Group (2-5)	2	2-3	3-5

Do not be fazed by the mention of calories and Kilojoules. These are the recommendations from the Food Pyramid and we will learn all about these later.

4. **Hypnosis**

The Use of Self Hypnosis as An Adjunct To The BTB PROGRAM
What is this? Black magic or mumbo jumbo?
Read on, O sceptic.

I am going to introduce a tool to you that will make your training program easier to fulfil and confer great health benefits upon you as well. This chapter will tell you all about it. It will tell you what it is, how it works, why it works and how to go about it.

Hypnosis
Look into my eyes...

Visions of black magic, some Rasputin like figure commanding you to do foolish or illegal actions?

Many people have fears about hypnosis and what it entails.
Will I wake up?
Won't I make a fool of myself? These and many other questions often spring to mind or are raised as concerns.

Hypnosis is safe and unlike medications does not have side effects. You can practice self hypnosis and apply it yourself to help you lose weight. This we will show you how to do. This also ensures safety as you decide what you need in your program.

In fact, no one can hypnotise you against your will or without your complete and willing cooperation. It depends entirely upon you, your intelligence and your powers of concentration.
Hypnosis is basically a relaxation technique that allows you to be in contact with and program your subconscious mind.

Hypnosis

The biggest drawback is the effectiveness after the hypnotic session. You probably have seen a stage hypnotist at work. They really are very good and skilful. About 11% of people are easily hypnotised so that in an audience the hypnotist will have enough satisfactory subjects. The hypnotist can get the subjects to do and believe many things whilst hypnotised but for our program the aim is to continue these beliefs and practises after the session.

You may not be one of these easily hypnotisable subjects but we believe that if you listen to a tape every day, the message will soon be imprinted in your subconscious mind and become part and parcel of your conscious life. The task book has instructions on the production of the tape.

Remember the old experiment conducted by Pavlov. Every time he fed dogs he rang a bell. Eventually he could get the dogs to salivate just by ringing the bell. The dogs had developed a conditioned reflex.

If you listen to this tape with concentration you too will condition yourself to the suggestions on the tape- these suggestions are to stick to your new eating pattern, to enjoy low calorie foods and be motivated to follow your training program.

What have you got to lose? Try it and see. One definite benefit will be invoking *the relaxation response*. This is the response whereby the body relaxes and down regulates or dissipates the effects of adrenalin and cortisone produced by your body's fright and flight response.

We all have a mechanism to help us escape from danger. When we are threatened e.g. being chased by a lion in days of yore we would pump out adrenalin and cortisone and other stress hormones, which results in the fright and flight response or fight and flight response. Our mouth is dry, our pulse races, blood flows through our muscles and is shunted away from our gut, our blood sugar rises as does our blood pressure. All these are very necessary to help us flee, run as fast as we can, climb a tree, scale a wall etc. We all have heard of amazing feats of strength and endurance when people are highly stressed. The physical action taken allows all these stress hormones to do their work and the energy is dissipated in a fruitful manner. In the modern era there are not many lions in the traditional form but they are there lurking in the bushes of modern-day life. The long traffic jams, hooting at robots, work stresses, interpersonal problems. They cause the same build up of stress hormones and energy but this is not dissipated as of old. More often than not there is neither sublimation nor release and the negative effects of raised blood pressure, raised muscle tension, raised blood sugar, increased stickiness of platelets etc all have deleterious effects upon the body. These can be offset by invoking the *relaxation response.* As Hypnosis is a form of relaxation therapy this will benefit your general health as well.

The instructions of how to make the tape will be found in the Task Book.

What then is Hypnosis?

Misconceptions about hypnosis abound. Many of these fallacies can be traced back to the unfortunate use of not-always-ethical demonstrations of hypnosis as a form of entertainment on stage and television. You probably have all seen someone being made to look silly and may have been put off by this demonstration of hypnosis.

This is exactly what hypnosis is NOT about. HAVE NO FEAR. We are going to use it professionally and in the beneficial way it is meant to be used.

WHAT IS HYPNOSIS?

We can define hypnosis as follows:

Hypnosis

***Hypnosis* is an induced state of altered consciousness in which communication with the subconscious mind is enhanced and suggestibility is increased.**

What does this mean?
Techniques are used to induce you into a state of relaxation of the body but heightened concentration of the mind.
Suggestions can be put to you that are incorporated in your subconscious mind so that they become part of your daily living. We will introduce you to the technique we suggest to achieve this state. You will apply it yourself and we can guarantee that it is safe. Before we get to the practical application we would just like to explore a little further the rationale behind hypnosis and how and why it works.

THE SUBCONSCIOUS AND THE HUMAN MIND
 The human brain has approximately one hundred billion neurons, and each neuron has about a thousand synapses, or connections to other neurons. That translates to something in the order of *one hundred trillion* connections in the brain. The electrochemical impulses that pass through these synapses are the foundation of all of our feelings, concepts, ideas, and all mental experiences.

There is growing evidence now that **the conscious mind**, as it is generally understood, is located in the **left-hand side of the brain** and the **subconscious mind** is located in **the right**. Each hemisphere has very different attributes or functions.

Our *conscious* mind, the left brain, processes information *logically* and *linearly*, literally in a straight line: 1, 2, 3, 4, 5, etc. It is *rational* and *organized*, and often referred to as the "analytic mind." The left brain also controls our voluntary (somatic) nervous system.
Our conscious mind helps with our daily decision-making processes

working according to the reality principle. It is intelligent, realistic, logical and proactive, especially in new situations where we have to apply rational thought processes to work out what to do and how to do it. However, it can only deal with between five and nine things at any one time and is easily overloaded.

The *subconscious* mind, or right brain, on the other hand, sees relationships in information and processes them in *random, abstract patterns*, even when pieces to the answer are missing. The right brain is *creative, intuitive, irrational,* and *emotional.* The right brain controls our involuntary (autonomic) nervous system.

Through *ideomotor* responses, or physical movements or behaviour in response to an idea or thought in the mind, we can speed up or slow down our heart, and even alter the chemical balance in our body to fight off disease.

The subconscious works on 'auto pilot' i.e. reacting according to the pleasure principle in that it seeks to avoid pain and obtain pleasure and survival, regardless of external considerations.

It is concerned with our emotions, imagination, and memories as well as our autonomic nervous system, which controls our internal organs automatically. These four main functions are very closely interlinked - in other words the mind affects the body and the body affects the mind. It is powerful and very clever at dealing with many complex instructions at any one time but is not 'intelligent'.

The two sides of our brain communicate with each other constantly, mixing logical, rational thoughts with the abstract and emotional, with emphasis in one hemisphere.

Mathematicians are generally left-brain people. Artists are generally right brain people. People of true genius know how to use both, with greater reliance on the right brain.

On the next page is a summary of these concepts of left and right brain.

Conscious Mind Left Brain	Unconscious Mind Right Brain
Logic	Recognition
Reason	Rhythm
Mathematics	Visual
Reading	Imagery
Writing	Creativity
Language	Synthesis
Analysis	Dreams
Ego	Symbols
	Emotions
	Id

Head Office
Where all the pro-active, logical, rational, planning thinking goes on.

Can only deal with 7 things (+/- 2) at any one time. Slow & subject to overload!

The Factory
Reacts very quickly to physical, emotional, real, imagined or remembered events. 24 hours.

Not always rational or appropriate!

Hypnosis

Among practitioners the most common view of hypnosis is that it is **an altered state of consciousness**; your awareness differs somehow to your everyday sense of reality. This is often referred to as **being in a trance.** However, for many, perhaps most, people being in hypnosis does not seem much different to how they feel at other times.

One difference such people do usually note, is that they feel relaxed. This has led to claims that hypnosis **is nothing more than profound relaxation.** But laboratory tests prove hypnosis is something more than relaxation: e.g. after hypnosis the heart rate remains slowed down longer than after relaxation alone.

Another definition holds that hypnosis is **a heightened state of suggestibility.** What does this mean? People in hypnosis will accept suggestions more readily than if not in hypnosis? That explains nothing. People are readily suggestible without hypnosis -- the mammoth advertising industry attests to that -- and people in hypnosis by definition want to cooperate. Of course they accept suggestions. They suspend their disbelief, as they would while reading a novel. But suggest something that is distasteful to them and they'll quickly stop cooperating -- just as they'd drop a novel which offended them.

Hypnosis has also been defined as **a form of conditioning.** A person learns, through direct experience or the media, how to behave 'hypnotised.' Another way to see hypnosis as something learned is to assert that a person becomes conditioned to a word stimulus such as "Relax." Once having allowed himself to relax, the client is thereafter conditioned to repeat the experience of relaxing upon hearing the stimulus-word.

Yet another definition of hypnosis is that it is **a form of dissociation.** That is, that in some as yet unexplained way, the mental functioning of a person is compartmentalised and one part can be isolated from the others.

Dissociation is an everyday conscious experience which begins in childhood. When a person is engaged in conversation with someone else he is also talking with himself and thinking ahead to his next comments. Children blithely slip in and out of fantasy lives, temporarily adopting make-believe roles, which they discard at will. This capacity to fantasize can be retained through practice and makes the dissociation characteristic of hypnosis less surprising.

It does not matter much whether hypnosis is an altered state, relaxation, heightened suggestibility, conditioning or dissociation. Hypnosis enables a person to experience thoughts and images as though they were real.

Hypnosis is like guided daydreaming: a form of relaxed concentration. What is relaxed is first the body and second, the conscious part of the mind.

UNCONSCIOUS HYPNOTISM

We often use self-suggestion in everyday life in the form of spontaneous thoughts or observations. Thoughts such as "I cannot stop smoking, no matter how hard I try", or "I'll never be able to do this" are often powerful but very negative self-suggestions.

We are also continually subjected to 'unconscious hypnotism' in our daily life by parents, teachers, peer pressure, politicians, etc. Newspaper and television advertising, for example, try to persuade us to do things e.g. buy a particular product. Repetition reinforces the suggestion. If you have ever found yourself at the checkout counter not knowing why you put something in the basket, this may be the reason.

If we are unaware of these negative suggestions we may cause ourselves all manner of disabilities or ailments. Thankfully suggestion is a two edged sword. Those who are instructed in its use can relieve the symptoms or unwanted behaviour patterns which negative suggestion may have caused.

This is really the great potential of the method we are going to use. Once you make your tape we want you to listen to it daily. The repetition of positive stimuli will make it more effective the more you practice it. Remember- practice makes perfect!

CONSCIOUS HYPNOSIS

Our subconscious mind often stubbornly prefers to cling on to known behaviours and symptoms even if they are negative and interfere with our peace of mind and quality of life. As far as it is concerned, change is potentially scary. In order to make positive changes and become mentally fit you must be consciously aware of the need for change, be motivated to get better, and be prepared to devote the time and effort necessary for doing the mental relaxation exercises. We all know that getting your body into shape involves more than merely thinking about going to the gym. Mental fitness calls for the same level of dedication.

We are training both your mind and your body- go to it. You can only benefit.

SELF-HYPNOSIS

It has been maintained that all hypnosis is essentially self-hypnosis. It is certainly impossible to be hypnotised by someone else unless you want or allow it to happen. Self-hypnosis is a way of safely bypassing the conscious mind. Once you have learned how to hypnotise yourself, practice will enable you to put yourself in a 'trance' whenever you wish to, quickly and easily.

Hypnosis, then, is a matter of *suggestibility*, of having the subject accept what you say as fact, of allowing you into their subconscious mind. *At that point, what you say is as real and genuine as any learned knowledge they have.*

We want to use hypnosis as a road into your subconscious mind. A good way to view hypnosis is as a state of intense relaxation and concentration, in which the mind becomes remote and detached from everyday cares and concerns. In this relaxed state the subconscious part of the mind is best able to respond creatively to suggestion and imagery. It can focus on the things you wish to change and on the ways you can best do so, free from analytical or anxious thoughts.

You are not asleep nor are you unconscious. You are in an altered or alternative state of consciousness in which you 'let things happen' through your subconscious mind rather than trying to make them happen with your conscious mind. Because you are deeply relaxed, the suggestions given to you by the hypnotist will be acted upon more easily by the subconscious. Posthypnotic suggestions are those that will be carried out by you when you come out of the hypnotic state.

Here you are going to listen to a pre-recorded tape at which will take you through a process, which will leave you hypnotized. I.e. in a state where suggestions will be made that you will be more receptive to. Messages will be left to be part and parcel of your day-to-day life so that it will be easier to stick to your programme. These will be; to be motivated to fill in your honesty book; no desire to snack inbetween meals; find low calorie food tasty and satisfying. Because you are making this tape recording you can add whatever you like at a later stage to accommodate your needs.

That, simply put, is how hypnosis works. In a hypnotized state, a subject told that a simple meal of salad and fruits is wonderfully tasteful and fully satisfying can easily call up the experience of good taste and satisfaction and believe it to be so. That person accepts the suggestion of satiety, because, first, we've removed the barriers the active conscious (logical) mind would put up. ("I don't like salad and it never fills me up), and second, our learned experiences about how you feel when you have had a satisfying meal can instantly be called upon to stimulate all the external senses we need to make the experience seem "real."

Our suggestions will be tailored to make day-to-day-living easier. We will suggest that you will find time each day to fill in your honesty book, listen to your tape and other thoughts that will help you complete a successful program.

People differ in their susceptibility to hypnosis. Approximately 11% of people are easily hypnotized and achieve this state of relaxation and heightened suggestibility easily and quickly. These are the people that stage hypnotists work with. There are always enough of them to be subjects. One has to concentrate intensely to be hypnotized and this people do when attending a stage show because they want to see what is going on.

The person being hypnotized must want to be hypnotized for you cannot hypnotize anyone against his or her will. The hypnotist is just someone who has a good technique and a convincing patter, which he or she can alter according to the response. He can also detect whether or not the process is affecting the person being hypnotized and adjust his technique accordingly. Most of you reading this book are not that easily hypnotized. That does not mean that you cannot benefit from the hypnotic techniques. Unlike the stage hypnotist we do not have to ensure that you are in the deepest stage or trance in ten minutes. We reckon that given enough time and commitment from your side almost anyone can be hypnotized. The greatest drawback in using hypnosis as an adjunct to therapy is the time it takes. This is not an issue here as, if you understand what we are up to and participate assiduously and enthusiastically, you too can gain these benefits. The wonderful thing about hypnosis is that there are no detrimental side effects or long-term effects. Your health will definitely benefit in any event because it is in essence a relaxation technique and the relaxation response is invoked each time you have a hypnotic session.

Hypnosis is not something one person "does" to another. Actually all hypnosis is self-hypnosis because it is the person who is being hypnotized who uses his or her abilities, including concentration and imagination, to produce what we recognize as "hypnotic" effects.

Hypnosis

Sound like a whole lot of mumbo jumbo to you?

If you have strong feelings and are not keen on this, you can follow the program omitting the hypnosis. However we would like you to seriously consider this technique, as we believe it will make it easier for you to stick to your new lifestyle. There are also added benefits in regularly invoking the relaxation response, as you will see when you read about this and stress.

We reiterate that the aim is to make you healthier, reduce your health risks and improve your quality of life. This hypnosis will do without side effects.

Still have doubts and are not convinced by what we have written above?

Consider this. Your hypnotic sessions are under your direct control. You will decide when and where they will occur. You will make the tape that you will use to induce the hypnotic state. You decide the content. The format we provide for you as an example but you are free to insert whatever makes you comfortable. We suggest that should you be disturbed you will immediately awaken and attend to the business at hand. We also suggest that you insert an admonition not to allow yourself to be hypnotized for any other reason other than a medical or dental reason.

Some folk worry that they will not wake from their hypnotic state. If one is deeply asleep or in a hypnotic state one will merely go off into a normal sleep and wake from this. If you are worried about this you can always set an alarm clock to wake you!

Nothing happens under hypnosis that does not happen in normal life. Scientists have performed many studies using different instruments and even measuring brain waves. There is neither magic nor any black magic. You cannot be made to do something against your will. Hypnosis is like many other forms of medical treatment- it works well for some and less well for others. We reckon however that the main reason why it does not work well for some is the time it takes to be effective. We are using it both as a technique to invoke the relaxation response with its health benefits and as an adjunct to making it easier to stick to your training program.

Hence- once again the old stuck needle admonition- "if you are seriously serious", and we believe you are if you have read this far, you will take the time and trouble and you will reap the benefits. One of the biggest plusses in using hypnosis is that the only side effect (the invoking of the relaxation response) is beneficial to your health. And that is not what one can say about many other medical interventions.

Remember also that you are your own hypnotist. You will make a recording of your own voice following a recipe we will give you. We do this because you would not be able to understand my accent if I sent you a tape recording. My broad South African accent is not the correct instrument to send you into a state of relaxation.

Making your hypnosis tape.
This is described in the Instruction section on page 115.

5.   Food. Energy Intake and Usage. Calories and Kilojoules.

Why do we eat?

We eat because we feel hungry.

This is Nature's way of telling you that you need food.

We need food to provide energy to keep our body functioning.

What happens to the food we eat?

As an example:

Let us look at what happens when we eat a peanut butter sandwich.

You chew this in your mouth where it is mixed with saliva and made into a form easy enough to swallow. This bolus of food moves from your mouth down your gullet and into your stomach. Here stomach acid and enzymes are added. All of these have an influence on the food as it passes through the body.

In the small intestine various juices and chemicals are added to this bolus, all intended to break down the sandwich to manageable bits. Once the sandwich is broken down into useful parts that the body can absorb, these are absorbed through the gut wall. They are transported via the bloodstream and the liver where they are processed and transported further to all the cells in the body that need them. The part of the sandwich that is not needed is passed on and out of the body via the large intestine, rectum and anus as waste products.

The peanut butter sandwich is a combination, for the most part, of carbohydrate (the bread) and fats and oils (the peanut butter), although it also has some protein, vitamins and minerals.

Food basically consists of

- **Carbohydrate**
- **Protein**
- **Fat**
- **Vitamins and minerals.**

Food. Energy Intake & Usage. Calories& Kilojoules.

All are necessary for the basic functioning of your body and for
growth, repair and maintenance.

The basic **energy needs** of the body are provided by carbohydrate
and fat.
Protein can provide energy sources but in the usual situation this is
minimal and proteins are mainly the building blocks of the body.
Food basically provides the energy necessary to power our bodies.
I.e. it is the fuel that allows us to live and go about our daily
business.

The old steam locomotives had to feed coal into their furnaces. This
heated water, which turned into steam that drove the pistons
making them work. You have to be mechanically minded to
understand how.
Food is the body's coal (source of energy).
Likewise you have to understand biochemistry and physiology to
understand how food we take in is absorbed and converted into
energy.

**It is not necessary however to understand all the intricacies if you
want to lose weight.**

We need a system that can tell us how much energy we are taking in
and how much we are using up. We use Calories (kilocalories) or
Kilojoules as the common system.

The Energy Value of Food
Our body requires energy to make it work. All the processes
necessary for life need energy. Thinking, talking and walking all
require energy as do the processes needed for absorbing food or
fighting off infection. Food provides us with this energy.
Carbohydrates, fats and proteins contain the energy that powers all
our biological functions. Exercise is one of the biological functions.

Food. Energy Intake & Usage. Calories& Kilojoules.

We can classify these in terms of a common factor: **energy**
Thus you can say carbohydrates contain "this" amount of energy
and doing a particular form of exercise requires "so much" energy
to perform.

Calories and Kilojoules

We need a common unit of measure so that we can speak the same
language.
How do we know how much weight a particular food will cause us
to put on- or in other words how much energy value it contains?
We can measure this energy as Calories.

The definition of a calorie is that it is the amount of heat necessary to
raise the temperature of 1 Kg (1 liter) of water 1 degree Celsius.

Thus a calorie is more accurately termed a kilogram calorie or
kilocalorie - abbreviated **kcal or Cal**
If we thus say that a particular foodstuff has a calorie value of 100 it
means that the energy trapped in the chemical bonds of this food, if
released would raise the temperature of 100 liters of water by 1
degree Celsius.
Scientists actually measure the energy values of different foodstuffs
in laboratories by placing it in a fancy instrument called a bomb
calorimeter. They add oxygen to this, ignite it with an electric
current, burn the food up completely and then measure the amount
of heat given off. This then gives the caloric value of the food.

The standard international unit for expressing energy is the joule or
kilojoule Kj
One Calorie or Kilocalorie = 4.2 Kilojoules.
The actual value is actually 4.186 kilojoules but we use the rounded
figure.

Food. Energy Intake & Usage. Calories& Kilojoules.

Why do we have two systems?

The world is trying to standardise to a metric system.

Whether this will ever happen, remains to be seen. Some countries use the one system and some the other.

The pros and cons of this argument are not for this book. We just have to put up with the frustration of different systems and terms for the same thing.

Use the system you are comfortable with and understand.

Below are some examples of the Energy Values of different foods

Food – 1 gram	Cals Kilocalories	Kilojoules
Alcohol	7	29
Carbohydrates	4	16
Protein	4	17
Fat	9	37
Dietary Fibre	3	13
Water	0	0

In truth Calories actually mean kilocalories. It is common usage that has added to the confusion.

The crucial point is to understand the facts below.

We can measure the energy value of the various types of food.

The unit of measurement of energy is calories (more correctly kilocalories) or kilojoules

1g of Carbohydrate provides 4 Kilocalories(Calories) or 16.8 Kilojoules of energy.

Whereas **1g of Fat provides 9 Kilocalories(Calories) or 37.8 Kilojoules of energy.**

Food. Energy Intake & Usage. Calories& Kilojoules.

By and large it is only Fat and Carbohydrate that provide energy for the body. Proteins are our building blocks and for the most part provide very little energy.

- If you take in more food than you need the excess is stored as fat
- If you take in less food than your body needs for its energy requirements, it has to mobilise its reserves of energy. These reserves of energy are stored as fat. When the body mobilises these reserves and they are used up the result is fat loss and thus weight loss.

Calculating the energy value of different foods allows us to compare them. Thus you can know how a meal at McDonalds, for instance, compares to a meal at home. How a bowl of ice cream compares in energy value to a bowl of fruit for example.
If you need **X** calories per day to perform your daily functions-and you take in **X** calories you will stay at the same weight.
If you take in more calories than you expend during a day the excess will be stored as fat.

If you use more calories than you ingest during a day, you will have to mobilise this energy from your stores i.e. fat. So you lose fat and lose weight.

Simple isn't it.

We eat food because this food provides us with energy, which makes us work. We use up this energy in going about our daily lives.

Food. Energy Intake & Usage. Calories& Kilojoules.

The energy we take in is used up by three processes:

1. **Our resting metabolism (The Resting metabolic rate)**
2. **The thermic effect of feeding**
3. **The thermic effect of exercise**

Big terms and complicated. Not really. Thermic means heat and we always talk of energy and heat. This is the energy burned up in doing the eating or the exercise.

The total daily energy expenditure depends upon
The resting metabolic rate 60-75%
Thermogenic effect of food consumed 10%
Energy spent during physical activity and recovery 15-30%

1. The Resting metabolic rate accounts for 60-75% of total daily energy expenditure.
This rate depends upon age, sex, body size, body composition, body temperature, thermogenic hormones and prior exercise.
This is energy required to keep your machine ticking over. This is the fuel required to keep you alive. All the systems that keep you alive like our heart and lungs and brain and kidney require energy to make them work. Energy is required for all the chemical processes taking place to keep you functioning.

2. The thermic effect of feeding accounts for about 10% of the daily energy expenditure.
This is the energy used after feeding. This is the energy necessary to digest, absorb and metabolise food.
The act of eating food sets a chain of reactions in place that result in energy expenditure- that is the process of eating and absorbing food from the gut into the bloodstream and transporting it to where this energy is needed at the cell level.

3. The thermic effect of exercise

This is the most variable component

This is the energy used in muscular activity (shivering, fidgeting, physical exercise.)

In sedentary humans it usually makes up about 15% of the daily energy expenditure.

If you train for 5-6 hours per day it can constitute up to 50% of your energy needs.

In sedentary people the amount of energy expended during exercise is usually under 100Kcal per day or 400 kilojoules

Yet endurance athletes can use up to 3000Kcal/day (12000Kj/day) in exercising.

Different people may expend energy at different rates. You may be a high or a low burner of energy- the resting metabolic rate may vary from 0.7Kcal/min to 1.6Kcal/min.

So it is true that some people just look at food and put on weight whereas others can eat what they like and still stay slim- whoever said life was fair! BUT you will not gain weight no matter what your metabolism is unless you eat more than YOUR own particular needs.

Exercise can enhance the resting metabolic rate but you need to exercise at an intensity of at least 50% of your VO2 max to do so. {VO2 max = your maximal oxygen consumption .i.e. when you are exercising as hard as you can.}

Palatability = (the degree to which food is liked)

Sweet tasting foods stimulate appetite. Hunger and energy depletion increase palatability. Satiety, nutrient loads and energy repletion decrease palatability.

Alteration of palatability helps to control meal size.

Food. Energy Intake & Usage. Calories& Kilojoules.

Fat is the most concentrated form of fuel we can consume and is metabolically the easiest to store.

A combination of easily absorbed carbohydrate and high fat produces a release of insulin which increases the activity of an enzyme (lipoprotein lipase) which accelerates the storage of fat. Foods that do this are for example doughnuts, chocolate, ice-cream, desserts.

That is: Sugary and rich in fat
= weight gain
= bad

When you are hungry even a plate of cabbage tastes great. When you are not hungry then vegetables don't taste wonderful but chocolate or a doughnut is easy to eat!

Once again if you expend more energy than you consume you will lose energy stores i.e. fat and hence weight.

Thus if you exercise more you will lose more weight.

It has also been shown that in overweight people the thermogenic effect of food consumed is less efficient than in slimmer people.

What should you be consuming each day?
The table below is a rough guide. In the task book we will show you how to calculate what you need to stay at the same weight. If you want to lose weight you have to take in less than this amount.

Food. Energy Intake & Usage. Calories& Kilojoules.

Gender	Age	Calories	Kilojoules
Men	23-50	2700	11340
Woman	23-50	2000	8400
Men	51-75	2400	10800
Women	51-75	1800	7560
Men	After 75	2050	8610
Women	After 75	1600	6720

Already you will be seeing that advice from different sources, gives different values. Compare the above with the stated facts in the Food Pyramid chapter. That is why in the instruction section we will show you how to work out what your own particular needs are.

Lets us recap some facts. There are only three ways in which your body uses the energy it obtains from food:
1. The basal energy requirements   Approx 70%
2. The thermogenic effect of food   Approx 10%
3. The energy expended during exercise   Approx 30%
This third category is really the one you can influence.

If you sit on your plonk each day and only exercise when you go to the dining room table or the kitchen for another doughnut you may only use as little as 5% of your energy expended during exercise. On the other hand if you have a very physical job such as bricklaying or you are training for and competing in triathlons, the energy expended in exercise may be 50% of your daily requirements.

But how much are you burning up during exercise?
There are all sorts of complicated ways of testing and formulas you can use. We will attempt to simplify this for practical every day use. This will sacrifice 100% accuracy for practicality but should not be too far off the truth. Below is a rough guideline

Weight in Kg	Light Exercise		Medium Exercise		Heavy Exercise	
	Cals per min	Kj	Cals per min	Kj	Cals per min	Kj
50	2	8	5	20	10	40
75	4	16	10	40	15	60
100	6	25	15	60	20	80

One thing to realise however is that merely by exercising alone you are **not** going to lose weight if you do not also address your food intake.
It definitely does help but if you also do not watch what you are eating you will not necessarily lose weight. It has even been found that training at an Olympic level is not enough to lose weight if you are overweight without considering your intake.
But most of us are not training at an Olympic level and exercising even less than these athletes.

How does calculating energy intake and expenditure help me?
You walk briskly for half an hour and you now think, "I have been exercising today so I can have two beers and a slab of chocolate.
Is this good reasoning? Assume you weigh 75 Kg.(165 lbs)
If you walk briskly for half an hour, this will use 450 calories or 1800

kilojoules.

Two beers represent 300 kilocalories or1350 kilojoules of energy intake and a slab of chocolate (45g bar) provides 250 kilocalories or 1050 kilojoules of energy. This is 550 Calories or 2800 kilojoules.

You have a negative balance of 100 calories or 420 Kilojoules

You thought you were doing well by exercising and could eat more but in fact you will gain over 10gm of fat if the above is what you did.

10gm extra per day translates into more than 3 Kg in a year.

Take home lesson:

- Exercise does not allow you to eat what you like.!!!!!

- You need to know the energy value of the various foods you ingest as well as the amount of energy you expend when exercising!

<u>Summary</u>

You don't need to quote the definitions or understand bomb calorimeters.

What you need to understand is that food provides energy. Your body uses this energy. Depending on your gender, age, weight and daily activities you need a certain amount of energy to complete your daily tasks.

We can work out how much energy you need.

This energy you obtain from your food.

The energy values of food are known.

We can work out how much energy the food you eat provides you.

We can also work out how much energy you use up in exercise.

At the end of the day if you have taken in more energy than your body needs it stores this as fat and you gain weight.

If you use more energy than your food supplies you with, your body mobilises fat and you lose weight.

Food. Energy Intake & Usage. Calories& Kilojoules.

The units of energy we use are:
- Calories, which is the same thing as a kilocalorie, or
- Kilojoules.

1 Calorie = 4.2 Kilojoules

6. **Portions, Weights and Measures**

How much is too much? How do you measure what you eat? How big is a cup? Grams, ounces, milliliters. All very confusing.
You cannot take a scale into a restaurant and measure what you are eating.
Our approach is to work out for yourself a system that will give you an idea of the amounts of food or energy you are ingesting.
The premise is that you gain weight because you are eating too much energy for your daily needs. This excess energy is then stored as fat and this is the reason for weight gain.
So you must measure what it is you eat and try to reduce this amount.
Thus we want you to measure in a simple fashion– our portions– and later on when you want to refine what you are doing, to measure more accurately.

Thus for starters **we define a portion** as:
For all foods except fats and sweets:
- The volume of one cup– 240ml or 8 oz {*note the size*}
- The area of the flat of your hand– not including your fingers and the thickness of your index finger
- The size of a tennis ball
- Two golf balls

For fats/oils and sweets a **portion** is a **tablespoon (Ts or Tbsp) or 15ml or 1/2 oz**

For liquids it's a **cup of 240ml or 8 oz.**

You need to check out the size of this cup and also a tablespoon. If you have an idea about these in your head you will be able to work out how many portions you take in every day.

59

Portions, Weights & Measures

Once again I must stress that the honesty book is central to this program. You don't know what you eat if you do not record it!

It is true that the surface of the flat of your hand may not be a standard size. There is a big difference between someone with a large hand and someone with a dainty little hand. It is also true that the large handed person will probably eat more than the tiny person due to the difference in size.

The most important is that these measurements are standard for you. If you know what you consider as a portion, that is fine, even if not scientifically accurate.

The plan is initially to see how many portions you ingest will leave you at the same weight.

You record the number of portions and your weight.

If you gain weight you reduce the number of portions by 10 percent until you even out.

Thus the program is individualized for you and it does not matter what size your hand is as long as you are consistent in estimating **YOUR** portions.

Then again you may feel uncomfortable that one portion of for e.g. chicken is not the same as a portion of rice or strawberries.

True– they are not and thus it is as we go along we try to show you the different energy values of different foods and different food groups.

Also that is why the sweets and fat and oil group has a portion of only 15ml or one tablespoon. This is the food group that contains the most energy value.

The program is structured so that progressively we become more accurate in assessing the energy values of different foods

Initially we sacrifice accuracy for simplicity. Eventually we try to get you to accurately work out what your energy needs are to stay at the same weight.

These will be recorded in your own calorie or kilojoule counter booklet.

There are many sources of information on the energy value of foods. Very few of them agree totally as regards values assigned to a food or food group. Thus you may find the one says a slice of bread is worth 100 calories and another that this is worth only 70. If you look on a loaf of bread's wrapping it may tell you that a slice of bread weighs 33gm whereas another will tell you their slice of bread weighs 30 grams.

The one may declare that the energy value is 77 Kilocalories and the other states that it is 90 Kilocalories.

Different companies have different values. This may well be true because the recipes vary. The one may have more oil than the next so the food energy value will be different. They are usually pretty accurate but sometimes are not.

You can go crazy worrying about a few discrepant calories here or there. The bottom line is to eventually end up with a set of values that you use and are standard FOR YOU.

This is not an exam that will be marked but a health exam that you have to pass. Thus it must work for you.

Use **your own standards** to balance your intake and output. It is no good to say that "I was taking what the book said and I still put on weight!" You have to work out what you need.

You will see that the values I have put on the portions of food groups are probably higher than in reality. Likewise the energy expenditure from the exercise is underestimated. If you are fastidious and want scientific accuracy, this can be achieved. What I want to achieve is for you to find out what in your eating pattern is causing the problem and to devise a strategy to overcome it.

So whatever works for you is fine. Just don't stress over the fact that there are different values almost everywhere you look. In your own book write down the values that work for you and use these.

Portions, Weights & Measures

The following is some detail about measurements that we usually use.

Measurement Equivalents

1 tablespoon (Tbsp) (Ts) = 3 teaspoons (tsp)(ts) =15 ml
1/16 cup (c) = 1 tablespoon
1/8 cup = 2 tablespoons
1/6 cup = 2 tablespoons + 2 teaspoons
1/4 cup = 4 tablespoons
1/3 cup = 5 tablespoons + 1 teaspoon
3/8 cup = 6 tablespoons
1/2 cup = 8 tablespoons
2/3 cup = 10 tablespoons + 2 teaspoons
3/4 cup = 12 tablespoons
1 cup = 48 teaspoons
1 cup= 16 tablespoons
8 fluid ounces (fl oz) = 1 cup = 240 ml
1 pint (pt) = 2 cups
1 quart (qt) = 2 pints
4 cups = 1 quart
1 gallon (gal) = 4 quarts
16 ounces (oz) = 1 pound (lb)
1 milliliter (ml) = 1 cubic centimeter (cc)
1 inch (in) = 2.54 centimeters (cm)

There is a difference between Fluid Ounces which is a volume measurement and Dry Ounces which is a weight measurement. Just to add to the confusion and frustration, in British, Australian and sometimes Canadian recipes, the imperial pint is used which is 20 fluid ounces in Britain. American and sometimes Canadian recipes use the American pint of 16 fluid ounces.
Not all tablespoons are the same. The Australian tablespoon is 20 ml; the British tablespoon is 17.7 ml.

Portions, Weights & Measures

In most Canadian recipes the tablespoon is 15 ml while the American tablespoon is actually 14.2 ml.

So if you are buying foods from all around the world you may become very frustrated if you are aiming for scientific accuracy. Throughout this book I have always sacrificed accuracy for practicality.
You often find that when you get down to the last parts of the program the different values can be frustrating. Then it may be of help to know accurately what the food value of your commonly chosen foods is. You can also check your "own" values by weighing foods when you have the time or inclination.
The following are some tables for those who want more detail.
Metric conversion factors Ts= Tablespoon ts =teaspoon   fl oz = fluid ounce

Multiply	By	To Get
Fluid Ounces	29.57	grams
Ounces (dry)	28.35	grams
Grams	0.0353	ounces
Grams	0.0022	pounds
Kilograms	2.21	pounds
Pounds	453.6	grams
Pounds	0.4536	kilograms
Quarts	0.946	liters
Quarts (dry)	67.2	cubic inches
Quarts (liquid)	57.7	cubic inches
Liters	1.0567	quarts
Gallons	3,785	cubic centimeters
Gallons	3.785	liters

Liquid or Volume Measures (approximate)			
1 ts		1/3 Ts	5 ml
1 Ts	1/2 fl oz	3 ts	15 ml 15 cc
2 Ts	1 fl oz	1/8 cup 6 ts	30 ml, 30 cc
1/4 cup	2 fl oz	4 Ts	59 ml
1/3 cup	2 2/3 fl oz	5 Ts 1 ts	79 ml
1/2 cup	4 fl oz	8 Ts	118 ml
2/3 cup	5 1/3 fl oz	10 Ts 2 ts	158 ml
3/4 cup	6 Fl oz	12 Ts	177 ml
7/8 cup	7 Fl oz	14 Ts	207 ml
1 cup	8 fl ozs 1/2 pint	16 Ts	237 ml
2 cups	16 fl ozs 1 pint	32 Ts	473 ml
4 cups	32 Fl ozs	1 quart	946 ml
1 pint	16 Fl ozs 1 pint	32 Ts	473 ml
2 pints	32 fl ozs	1 quart	946 ml 0.946 liters
8 pints	1 gallon 128 fl oz	4 quarts	3785 ml 3.78 liters
4 quarts	1 gallon 128 fl oz	1 gallon	3785 ml 3.78 liters
1 liter	1.057 quarts		1000 ml
128 fl oz	1 gallon	4 quarts	3785 ml 3.78 liters

Dry or Weight Measurements (Approximate)

1 ounce		30 grams (28.35 g)
2 ounces		55 grams
3 ounces		85 grams
4 ounces	1/4 pound	125 grams
8 ounces	1/2 pound	240 grams
12 ounces	3/4 pound	375 grams
16 ounces	1 pound	454 grams
32 ounces	2 pounds	907 grams
1 kilogram	2.2 pounds/ 35.2 ounces	1000 gram

7.   Medications and Surgery for Weight Loss.

If there was a simple method for losing weight, there would be no overweight people.

If taking a pill would help you achieve your ideal weight, there would be no need for this program and you would not be reading this.

Many methods have been tried and the results are to summarise– disappointing.

Yes there are some benefits and the above can be used as adjuncts but they are not wonder cures.

Many drugs have been touted as effective in producing weight loss and many have come and gone over the years.

Many have been banned or discontinued in medical circles due to unacceptable side effects.

This is not a treatise on all that is available.

My advice is that you should only consider these methods after thorough discussion with a trusted health care practitioner.

Many so called natural products contain diuretics, laxatives and other potentially harmful substances.

If you go, even to a health shop, and purchase something that is in a plastic bottle and is presented in capsules, this is not "natural" as it has been produced in a factory somewhere. Natural does not necessarily mean safe.

I also strongly advise you not to take anything that does not have the ingredients marked clearly on the packaging or has been vetted by your doctor. There are also many sites on the internet making fabulous claims for various potions and pills. Those that do not have the ingredients clearly marked on them cannot be verified as to safety. Those that do not have FDA or another drug safety regulatory body's approval or a disclaimer that "this product does not have FDA approval" should be viewed with suspicion. FDA= US food and Drug Administration.

In any event the basis of weight loss is a new eating pattern and any medications used are merely to aid this goal.

Before taking them the following questions should be posed and answered:

- How much weight loss can I expect when using this medication?
- Will the weight loss be sustained?
- Are there any side effects when taking this medication?
- What is the cost and for how long should I take it?

In March of 2005 I reviewed the medical literature to obtain an update of the benefits of medication used for weight loss. These are medications deemed suitable for use by medical practitioners and where there is strong scientific evidence that they work.

Here follows a selection of some of the medical literature that is available on the subject.

Now this may not be everyone's cup of tea and may have too much medicalese for your liking. I record it below but do summarise it at the end so if you find this too much, skip it and go on to the summary.

Glazer G. Long-term pharmacotherapy of obesity 2000: a review of efficacy and safety. Arch Intern Med. 2001 Aug 13-27;161(15):1814-24.

Weight loss attributable to obesity pharmacotherapy (i.e., in excess of placebo) in trials lasting 36 to 52 weeks was 8.1% or 7.9 kg for those receiving phentermine resin, 5.0 % or 4.3 kg for those receiving sibutramine hydrochloride, 3.4% or 3.4 kg for those receiving orlistat, and -1.5% or -1.5 kg for those receiving diethylpropion hydrochloride. Physiologic, pathologic, and epidemiological studies strongly support that anorexiant-induced valvulopathy is attributable to specific serotonergic properties of the fenfluramines that are not present with available weight loss drugs.

Phentermine = Ionamin Adipex-P

Sibutramine = Meridia

Orlistat = Xenical
Diethylpropion =Tenuate and Tenuate dospan

Phentermine is the most commonly prescribed prescription appetite suppressant, accounting for 50% of the prescriptions.
Phentermine first received approval from the Food and Drug Administration (FDA) in 1959 as an appetite suppressant for the short-term treatment of obesity.
Phentermine resin became available in the United States in 1959 and Phentermine Hydrochloride in the early 1970s.
In the US, Phentermine is currently sold under the brand names Ionamin® (Medeva Pharmaceuticals) and Adipex-P® (Gate Pharmaceuticals). It is also available as a generic medication, known as 'phentermine'.
Previously, it was sold under the name Fastin® (formerly produced by King Pharmaceuticals for SmithKline Beecham). In December 1998, SK-Beecham withdrew Fastin from the market.

FEN-PHEN (or Phen-Fen) and Dexfen-Phen - two passing trends
Fen-Phen refers to the combination, or cocktail, of Fenfluramine or Pondimin (the "Fen") and Phentermine (the "Phen"). Fenfluramine received FDA approval in 1973 for the short-term treatment of obesity. Together, Phentermine and Fenfluramine produced a powerful diet drug cocktail.The FDA never approved the Fen-Phen combination, but once the agency has approved a drug, doctors may prescribe it at will.
Their use, together, was considered "off-label".
By the summer of 1997, the Mayo Clinic reported 24 cases of heart valve disease. All 24 people had taken the Fen-Phen cocktail. The cluster of unusual cases of heart valve disease in Fen-Phen users suggested a co-relation between Fen-Phen use and heart valve disease.
Further evaluations of patients taking Fenfluramine or Dexfenfluramine, showed that approximately 30% had abnormal

valve findings. This figure is much higher than expected for abnormal test results and suggest Fenfluramine and Dexfenfluramine as the likely causes of Primary Pulmonary Hypertension (PPH) and valvular heart disease.

The FDA responded promptly to the alarming findings, and in September 1997, requested drug manufacturers to voluntarily withdraw Fenfluramine and Dexfenfluramine. At the same time, the FDA recommended that patients using either Fenfluramine or Dexfenfluramine stop taking them.

Padwal R, Li SK, Lau DC. Long-term pharmacotherapy for obesity and overweight. Cochrane Database Syst Rev. 2004; (3):CD004094. Of the eight anti-obesity agents investigated, only orlistat and sibutramine trials met inclusion criteria. Attrition rates averaged 33% during the weight loss phase of orlistat trials and 43% in sibutramine studies. All patients received lifestyle modification as a co-intervention. Compared to placebo, orlistat-treated patients lost 2.7 kg (95% CI: 2.3 kg to 3.1 kg) or 2.9% (95% CI: 2.3 % to 3.4%) more weight and patients on sibutramine experienced 4.3 kg (95% CI: 3.6 kg to 4.9 kg) or 4.6% (95% CI: 3.8% to 5.4%) greater weight loss. The number of patients achieving ten percent or greater weight loss was 12% (95% CI: 8% to 16%) higher with orlistat and 15% (95% CI: 4% to 27%) higher with sibutramine therapy. Weight loss maintenance results were similar. Orlistat caused gastrointestinal side effects and sibutramine was associated with small increases in blood pressure and pulse rate.

REVIEWER'S CONCLUSIONS: Studies evaluating the long-term efficacy of anti-obesity agents are limited to orlistat and sibutramine. Both drugs appear modestly effective in promoting weight loss; however, interpretation is limited by high attrition rates.

What do these fancy statistics mean?
Compared to placebo you only lose 2.7 Kg of weight when you use orlistat and 4.3 kg for sibutramine

Only 12% of subjects on orlistat lose more than 10% of their weight and only 15% on sibutramine lose 10% or more of their weight. Nearly 1/3-1/2 of the patients do not complete the trials. These reviewers think that the trials done on the other drugs are of too poor a quality to comment upon. All the other literature is similar so I won't repeat it.

The bottom line is that you may be one of the fortunate ones and gain benefits BUT the majority of people do not and the benefits are usually modest. Then again there are the added considerations of cost and of side effects. If you are going to use medications, I repeat that I think you should do this on the advice and under the supervision of your doctor.

Surgery for weight loss

This is generally called bariatric surgery and a variety of procedures are performed from efforts to reduce the size of the stomache (e.g. gastric banding, stapling etc to more complicated bypass operations or bowel resections.) Great results are claimed for these operations and they can have some health benefits. As I stated in the beginning overweight people are more at risk when they undergo surgery. This is true also for this surgery and it is by no means a quick fix. This is not a decision to be taken lightly and should not be done so without close advice from a trusted health care worker. It should also be undertaken together with a plan for reducing food intake in any event. I performed a literature search of reputable medical journals to look at the efficacy and safety of these operations. This I performed in March of 2005 and you must remember that the research presented is usually that from major units and academic centres. This is my summary of what I found. I tried to be as unbiased as I could be to see really what the value of these procedures is.

My comments.

What are you hoping for?-the ideal weight – don't fool yourself.
Good results are if you lose 50 % of your *excess weight* and after a
few years most still regain weight above this 50% loss
It seems as there is a death rate at operation or in the first 30 days of
between 1/100 to 1/1000 depending upon the procedure performed
and 25 % have complications. These are not small complications and
requires re-operation in many instances
10 -25% require re-operation for inadequate weight loss.
There is no such thing as "just a small operation". Even the so called
minor surgical procedures have complication and death rates
although not as great as the more complex procedures. The more
complex the procedure the greater the weight loss but also the
greater the chances of complications.
There are also significant after effects such as frequent and loose
stools, bloating, gas and discomfort. Many procedures require
monitoring clinically and with blood tests and many other
investigations after the procedure. Comments are made by the brave
surgeons who report their figures- That the learning curve of this
surgery is long and steep.

Complications are more common in surgeons learning the
techniques. One study suggests a learning curve of between 150-200
operations.
And these are figures of reported surgery- What about the surgeons
who are performing this with early experience or do not report poor
results?
The above figures are rather frightening if this is for the successful
surgery.
So before considering surgery, please ask yourself;
- Why are you doing this?
- What do you expect?

- Is it worth the risk?
- Does the surgeon who is performing the operation keep statistics of his success and failure rates?
- Is he or she willing to discuss this with you?

In any event surgery will be more successful if it goes together with a healthy lifestyle program.

8.   Health Benefits of Exercise

A few questions are often asked about exercise.
- What are the benefits in taking regular exercise?
- Can exercise be harmful?
- What are the dangers in exercising?
- How much or how little exercise is beneficial to health?

What follows here are some facts gained from medical literarature I have accessed. I first wrote an article which had 74 references about the facts. I was soon put in my place about this article and told to edit it severely. Suffice it to say that all the facts below have been offered in reputable medical journals and atricles and references can be provided if you want the detail.

Studies show encouraging associations between exercise activity and good health.
Benefits are the greatest in elderly, sedentary and obese populations because the detrimental health related consequences of extreme inactivity are rapidly reversed. The greatest benefits are achieved when the least active individuals become moderately active.

Much less benefit is apparent when the already active individual becomes extremely active.

Physical activity that appears to provide the most health benefits is that where large muscles groups are used in weight bearing activity at a moderate intensity. That is, for example, walking, running or jogging.

Overexertion or inappropriate exercise can produce significant health risks.

Health Benefits of Exercise

Health benefits may also occur by the frequent performance of low intensity exercise which is inadequate for increasing fitness. You may not be fit enough to run a marathon but there are definite benefits to your health.

Exercise can also provide psychological benefits.

Exercise can increase longevity and improve overall health and quality of life.

At any age, changes in behaviour, quitting cigarette smoking, controlling blood pressure and becoming physically active, act independently to delay or decrease mortality and extend life.

What are the benefits of exercising?

AGEING AND PHYSIOLOGICAL FUNCTION

Performance measures improve during childhood and reach a maximum between late teens and thirty years of age.
Functional capacity declines with age. Deterioration varies widely according to lifestyle characteristics.
Different functions decline at different rates .

- Nerve conduction velocity decreases only 10-15% from 30-80 years of age.
- Maximum breathing capacity decreases by 60% in the same age group.
- Heart rate at rest does not change much with ageing, but shows an appreciable decline during maximal exercise.

Ageing effects are greatly influenced by regular exercise.
Exercising vigorously when you are young does not confer those same benefits as exercising throughout your life.

Health Benefits of Exercise

Aerobic capacity is approximately 25% higher in each age category amongst active people than sedentary people.

Muscular strength is highest for men and women between the age of 20 and 30 years. Thereafter strength declines slowly at first and then more rapidly after middle age. Strength loss amongst elderly is directly associated with their limited mobility and physical performance as well as to increases in incidence of falls.

There is a 40-50 % reduction in muscle mass between 25 and 80 years of age due to motor unit losses and muscle fibre atrophy. This decrease in musculoskeletal mass and strength that occurs with ageing is the combined result of progressive neuromotor processes and decrease in the daily level of muscle loading

Marked and rapid improvement can be achieved with vigorous training into the ninth decade of life.

In older men and women exercise training, particularly resistance training, facilitates protein synthesis and retention and blunts the inevitable loss of muscle mass and strength with ageing.

EFFECT OF AGEING ON NEURAL FUNCTION- nervous system
There is a 37% decline in the number of spinal cord axons and a 10% decline in nerve conduction velocity. Active groups of people move significantly faster than a corresponding age or group that are less physically active. An active lifestyle may positively affect neuromuscular funtioning at any age. Older men who have remained active for 20 years or longer have reaction times that are equal to or faster than inactive men in their 20's.

EFFECTS OF AGEING ON PULMONARY(Lung)FUNCTION
All measures of lung function generally deteriorate with age. A lifetime of regular physical activity may retard the decline in pulmonary function associated with ageing. Values for various

medical measurements such as vital capacity, total lung capacity, residual lung volume, maximum voluntary ventilation, FEV1 and FEV1/FVC in athletes older than 60 years of age are consistantlly larger than expected based on their body size and significantly larger than those of sedentary age matched healthy counterparts.

THE EFFECT OF AGEING ON CARDIOVASCULAR FUNCTION
Aerobic Capacity:

Data indicates that VO2 max. declines about 1% each year in adults. (VO2 Max is a complicated concept to understand but simplistically is an individual's maximal capacity to do work aerobically. It is one measurement of how well your heart, blood vessels and muscles function.)

Sedentary men and women have nearly a two-fold faster rate of decline in VO2 max. as they age and some research has actually shown no decline in aerobic capacity for individuals who have maintained relative constant training during a ten year period.

Becoming overfat and sedentary accelerate the rate of decline.

EFFECT OF EXERCISE ON HEART RATE
No significant change in resting heart rate occurs with ageing. The maximum hert rate with exercise does decline with age. A rough approximation of the maximal heart rate with age is the following:

- Maximum heart rate beats per minute is 220 minus your age in years

Cardiac output declines with age because of a lower maximum heart rate. Contributing to reduced capacity for blood flow is a reduction in the heart stroke volume which may account for as much as 50% of the age related decline in VO2 max. Accompanying the age related decrease in muscle mass is a reduction in peripheral blood flow capacity. This is probably the result of decrease in the capillary to muscle fibre ratio and a reduction in the arterial cross sectional area.

LIFESTYLE OR AGEING

The degree to which cardiovascular function decline is a direct result of ageing or a lack of habitual physical activity has not been precisely determined. Currently it is believed that sedentary living may cause losses in functional capacity that are at least as great as the effects of ageing itself.

There is a high degree of trainability amongst older men and women. Skeletal muscle, substrate metabolism and cardiovascular adaptions are similar to those of younger counterparts.

Low and high intensity regular exercise enables older individuals to retain cardiovascular functioning much above age-paired sedentary subjects of the same age.

When previously active middle aged men followed a regular endurance exercise programme over a ten year period the usual 9-15% decline in work capacity and maximal aerobic power was forestalled. At age 55 these active men had maintained the same values for blood pressure, body mass and VO2 max as they had at 45 years of age.

Among elderly individuals, exercise training can enhance the heart's systolic and diastolic properties and increase aerobic capacity to the same relative degree as in younger adults.

The effect of age on body composition.

After 35 years of age men and women tend to progressively gain body fat until the fifth or sixth decade of life. After sixty years of age total body mass is reduced, despite a decreasing level of body fat. Although it is common for most adults to grow fatter as they age, those who engage in heavy resitance training increase their lean body mass and decrease body fat.

Bone mass.
Osteoporosis is a major problem of ageing, particularly amongst postmenopausal women. This condition results in a loss of bone mass as the ageing skeleton becomes demineralised and porous. At the age of sixty the reduction in bone mass can be between 30 and 50% in certain people.

Trainability and age:
Regular moderate to vigorous physical activity produces physiological improvements regardless of age. When a healthy person, young or old, is given an appropriate training stimulus large and rapid improvement in physiological function occurs, often at a rate and magnitude that is independent of the person's age.

Healthy older people show no negative metabolic or hormonal responses or maladaptations to regular exercise, that would contraindicate participation in a standard exercise training programme.

EXERCISE AND LONGEVITY
Former Harvard oarsmen exceeded their predicted longevity by 5.1 years.
Participation in athletics as a young adult does not necessarily ensure increased longevity
However significant protection is provided for health and longevity if physical activity is maintained throughout life.

The results of longterm studies can be summarised as follows:
1. Regular exercise countered the lifeshortening effects of cigarette smoking and excess body mass.

2. Even people with hypertension who exercised regularly reduced their death rate by one half.
3. Even genetic tendencies towards early death were countered by regular exercise. For individuals who had one or both parents die before the age of 65 years, which is a significant health risk, a lifestyle that included regular exercise reduced the risk of death by 25%.
    A 50% reduction in mortality rate was observed for those active men whose parents lived beyond 65 years.
4. The persons who exercised more had improved health profiles. Mortality rates were 21% lower for men who walked 9 or more miles(14.5 Km) per week, than men who walked 3 miles(4.8 km) or less.
5. Life expectancy was increased in men who performed the equivalent of light sport activity compared to men who remained sedentary.
6. The life expectancy of Harvard alumni increased steadily from an exercise energy expenditure of 500Kcals per week to 3,500 Kcals – a value equivalent of 6-8 hrs of strenuous weekly exercise.
7. In addition the active men lived an average of 1-2 years longer than sedentary class mates. Beyond weekly exercise of 3500 Kcal there were no additional health or longevity benefits.

When exercise was carried to extremes, the men had higher death rates than the more moderately active colleagues.

From available data it seems that, if life extending benefits of exercise exist, they are associated more with the prevention of early mortality and an improvement of overall life span.

Although the maximum lifespan may not be extended greatly, more active people tend to have a ripe old age.

Health Benefits of Exercise

Interestingly enough *only light to moderate regular activity such as walking, gardening, stair climbing, household chores is needed to achieve positive health benefits for previously sedentary men and women.* Clearly there is a strong association between lack of regular physical activity and physical fitness and all causes of death. The greatest impact was noted for diseases of the cardiovascular system. Even the modest amount of regular exercise substantially reduced the risk from dying of heart disease, cancer and other causes.

Relatively low levels of both physical activity and fitness offer significant protection.

Engaging in just light to moderate regular exercise provides significant protection although the greatest benefits are noted in more vigorous exercising. The risk to longevity associated with sedentary lifestyle was as great as smoking one pack of cigarettes per day or being 20% overweight.
There is excellent and strong evidence that exercise is beneficial in the following conditions:
All cause mortality i.e. if you exercise you add years to your life, Coronary artery disease, Hypertension ,Obesity, Diabetes, Osteoporosis and functional capacity.

There is some evidence that exercise may be beneficial in the following conditions; stroke, breast disease, prostate, colon and lung cancer

IS EXERCISING SAFE?
People worry about exercising because of publicised reports of sudden death during exercise. This rate has declined over the past 25 years despite an overall increase in exercise participation.
In one report of cardiovascular episodes during 65 months, 2 935 exercisers recorded 374 798 hours of exercise that included 2 ,726,

272 Kms of running and walking. There were no deaths during this time and only two non fatal cardiovascular complications.

This amounted to *2 complications per 100 000 hours of exercise for women and 3 complications for men.*

Heavy physical exertion provides a small risk of sudden death during the activity when comparied to resting for an equivalent time, especially for sedentary people. Therefore if you are not fit or generally active and you want to start exercising, DO IT VERY SLOWLY AND GRADUALLY!
The longer term health benefits of regular exercise far outway any potential for acute cardiovascular complications.
Considerably less risk of death exists during exercise among people who are regularly physically active
The likelihood of an exercise catastrophe eg. Stroke, aortic dissection and rupture, lethal arrhythmias, myocardial infarction increase under the following conditions
1.   Family history of sudden death at young age.
2.   History of fainting or chest pain with exercise.
3.   Unaccustomed vigorous exercise.
4.   Exercise performed with accompanying psychological stress.
5.   Extremes of environmental temperature.
6.   Exercise involving a significant straining or static muscle action component.
7.   Exercise during viral infection or when not feeling well.

The most prevalent exercise complications are musculo-skeletal injuries. For running activities the greatest orthopoedic injury occurs in individuals who exercise for extended periods.
There you have it. Exercise is safe! If you use your common sense it is not dangerous.

How much exercise do you need to do for health benefits?
Current public health recommendations for physical activity are for 30 min of moderate-intensity activity each day, which provides substantial benefits across a broad range of health outcomes for sedentary adults.

Persons who get 30 min of moderate-intensity exercise per day are likely to achieve additional health benefits if they exercise more.

In addition to aerobic exercise, people should engage in resistance training and flexibility exercises at least twice a week, which will promote the maintenance of lean body mass, improvements in muscular strength and endurance, and preservation of function, all of which enable long-term participation in regular physical activity and promote quality of life

Any type of physical activity is better than no activity for protection against functional limitations, but exercise confers greater benefit for physical capacity.

For the effects to persist, physical activity must be regular.

The effects may persist when the duration and frequency of exercise is slightly reduced, particularly if the intensity remains the same.

Physical activity is the best and most significant way of ensuring the maintenance of functional capacity. Physical activity is therefore especially important in the prevention of the detrimental effects of ageing and chronic illnesses.
Excessive or incorrect exercise may disturb vital functions, cause stress disorders or injuries. The margin between suitable and excessive exercise (i.e. the therapeutic range of physical activity) may be narrow, particularly in those in poor health.

Health Benefits of Exercise

Your heart rate during exercise should be approximately **60-75 % of your maximum heart rate**. This type of exercise, for example brisk walking, is considered to be **moderately intense.**

Your maximum heart rate is 220 - your age in years

To improve cardiovascular fitness, physical activity needs to include rhythmic movements of the large muscle groups which should be sustained for a considerable length of time (usually several tens of minutes). Walking, cross-country skiing, cycling and swimming are examples of endurance (stamina) building exercise.

Multiple short periods of exercise (multiples of 10 minutes) are as beneficial as a single long period (40 minutes) in terms of weight loss and fitness (in combination with dietary change).

Get breathless more often. You don't have to go to a gym or be an Olympic marathon runner. Simply walking a mile(1 ½ Km a day, or taking reasonable exercise three times a week (enough to make you sweat or glow) will substantially reduce the risk of heart disease. If you walk, don't dawdle. Make it a brisk pace.

MOST IMPORTANT-YOU DONT HAVE TO EXERCISE AS IF TRAINING FOR A MARATHON. Moderate exercise will give you the same health benefits as if you did.

How do you start exercising? The secret is: **go slow, start low.**

Do not do too much too soon.

The idea is a gradual increase in exercise. The training effect is adaptation to increasing levels of exercise. Our aim is to gain health benefits from the exercise- not to train you for the next Olympics.

Remember: The only way to slow the ageing process is by exercising.

Health Benefits of Exercise

We are aiming to put life in your years. There is no age and no state of unfitness that will not benefit from increasing exercise. This of course presupposes that you do not have a medical condition in which exercise is contraindicated.

It sounds ridiculous to only do 5 minutes but I have found this a good way of getting into exercise. Start by doing 5 minutes per day until you can manage this with no discomfort for a week: then you increase it to 7 minutes per day for a week.

The following week you increase this to 12 minutes then 15 minutes per day and so on.

The idea is slowly building up the amount you do and gaining the health benefits. Remember training is the progressive adaptation to increased stress.

Choose an exercise that you enjoy. There are many discarded treadmills and stationary cycles that were purchased at the beginning of an exercise program. Don't purchase these unless you enjoy doing these forms of exercise. You are far more likely to continue exercising if you partake in an activity you enjoy.

The Energy used in Exercising

The conditioning and the calories burned during exercise are directly related to the duration and intensity of that exercise. The harder you work, the more calories you burn up. If you use up energy, you are getting rid of fat.

The next table has some examples of calories burned during 30 minutes of activity:

Each half an hour of exercise will burn up approximately

Type of exercise 30 mins	Kilocals Cals	Kilojoules Kj
Brisk Walking	200	840
Strenuous exercise	500	2100
Jogging 9min/mile 6 min/km	380	1600
Swimming	250	1050
Bicycling	200	840
Water aerobics	200	840
Aerobics	300	1260
Squash/raquetball	300	1260
Tennis	200	840
Aerobic dancing	250	1050
Bowling	100	420
Calisthenics	225	945
Sexual intercourse	100	420
Dancing	150	630

Health Benefits of Exercise

Desk work	75	315
Football (touch)	300	1260
Golf (using power cart)	100	420
Golf (walking)	200	840
Walking at 2 mph/3.2Km/h	75	315
Walking at 4 mph/6.4km/h	160	672

Summary:
There seems to be good evidence that physical fitness and exercise can give definite health benefits at all age groups. The thing we need to be stressing is that the amount of exercise needed is not excessive and is well within the capabilities of all people. For health benefits more is not necessarily better and a half an hour of brisk walking each day will do wonders for your health at all ages.

You will even gain health benefits from modest exercise of 30 minutes three times a week where you are performing moderately hard exercise. This can also be broken up into periods of 10 minutes so no –one can ever say they have "no time to exercise". This may not make you fit but does have positive health benefits.
It does not help that you were the champion athlete at school. The benefits are there but only if you continue exercising for life. Even though you can add a few years to your life by exercising the biggest benefit seems to be that you *add life to your years* i.e. a better quality of life.

Do you exercise regularly?

9. What should you drink?

The obvious answer to this is something that contains the lowest amount of calories. *Water contains absolutely no calories* and if one can train oneself to drink this, then this is ideal. However many people find this unsatisfactory. *Most of the diet drinks also have no calories.*

Contrast this with the calorie content of the following common drinks.

Drink	Oz	Ml	Cals	Kj
Spirits	1	30	80	340
Beer Light	12	360	100	420
Beer non alcohol	12	360	80	340
Beer	12	360	150	630
Wine	3.5 1 glass	100	80	340
Soda	12	360	150	630
Synthetic fruit juice	12	360	150	630
Diet drinks	12	360	<1	<5
Water	12	360	0	0

10.   Why am I gaining weight?

Every day I am asked this question." Doctor, why am I gaining weight? I do not each much at all! For breakfast I have …. And for lunch…. "

And so it goes.

You don't have to eat much at all to gain weight. If you, for instance, take in 1 slice of bread with butter and honey more than your daily needs this represents a gain of 170 Cals per day (100 +20+50) = 18.8 gms per day = 566 gms per month = 6.8 Kg per year

Over 10 years this equates to 68 Kgs extra weight.

The only way you will know what you take in is to record it and that is why the honesty book is crucial to the program.

"Is it not my glands, doctor?"

This is another frequent question.

Of course it may be but the endocrine or other causes of weight gain are pretty rare and unusual.

There are some medical conditions that can make it more difficult to lose weight and can even aggravate weight gain. There are also some medications that can promote weight gain. That is why we suggest you are assessed by your doctor to evaluate these and exclude all the causes that also need to be managed.

Irrespective of the cause of your weight gain– even if it is medical, part of the management is to restrict your intake. The only way you will lose weight is to take in less energy than YOUR body, with it's own particular set of circumstances, needs.

Look at the TV when the news is on about a famine somewhere or about a poor area. Often the only overweight people you may see are the politicians. The average person with no access to food or someone who cannot afford enough food, is thin and underweight.

Why am I gaining weight?

Now in these populations there must also be these medical causes (thyroid and adrenal gland disease etc) but we don't see the overweight people.

The basic cause of weight gain is accessibility to food and being able to afford it.
So perhaps the major reasons are access, affordability and taking in more than YOUR body needs.
The amount your body needs depends upon your age, gender, underlying medical conditions, rate of metabolism, daily activities, lifestyle and many other factors.
Genetics also plays a role and we all know people who can eat what they like but still not put on weight.
However unfair that may seem, it does not help your problem. You have to deal with your set of circumstances and address the issues that will help you.
So, whatever your medical condition, attention to eating and exercise patterns are also crucial.
The sad thing about the world is that there are as many overweight people in the world as there are underweight or undernourished people.
In the first world countries life expectancies have been on the increase with the major reason being better nutrition, housing, access to clean and safe water as well as access to medical care.
However predictions are that the health parameters and life expectancies will drop in these countries due to the epidemic of overweight and the medical problems that go with this condition–diabetes, hypertension, heart and vascular disease amongst others.

We don't want you to be one of these statistics!

11. How quickly should I lose weight?

This depends upon you and what you want to achieve and how badly you want to achieve this.

From the beginning I have nattered on about how this is only for the seriously serious and that it is not easy nor a quick fix. There is just no way that you can lose weight very swiftly without significant health risks and with the problem that it will quickly return if you take abnormal lengths to lose weight.

So in this program you will not find a false claim about how swiftly you will lose 10 kg or achieve an ideal weight.

Instead I will show you what is attainable, how to attain this and then you can see how quickly **you** want to achieve your goals.

My goals for you are improved health together with weight loss.

Attaining an ideal weight?

Nowhere in this program will you see an ideal weight nor a target weight. I don't believe in these as many of these are unrealistic. I believe you must aim for health and quality of life.

As you have seen our bodies change shape as we age and muscle is replaced by fat. The middle-age spread is no myth. Thus the ideal weight of a 60 year old is not the same as that of a 17 year old. If you are very muscular you may appear overweight on some tables. Your health status should be assessed by your doctor and he or she may talk of your BMI or body mass index as a measure of your healthy body weight.

So my advice is to ask your doctor as the health assessment is more than just weight.

How quickly should I lose weight?

Most of weight gain does not occur overnight yet most people who want to lose weight want to do this as quickly as possible. If this is what you want you are almost certainly going to be disappointed. Disappointment leads to disillusionment and giving up. This program aims to put you on the road to health. I don't want you to aim for a quick fix but rather a permanent fix.

I am very happy if my patients who need to lose weight do so at a rate of ONE, yes ONE, kilogram a month.

If this is combined with a new healthy lifestyle which includes exercise, I can guarantee that their health will be improved and all the parameters we measure- Blood pressure, cholesterol, weight, blood sugar will show improvement.

And if you think about it—over one year this person losing one kilogram per month will have lost 12 kilograms, which is a lot of weight. What is more, it is likely to stay off as it goes with a new approach to life and health.

Let us just look at a practical example:

A woman weighs 60 kg and would like to weigh 55 kg
Estimated current kilojoule intake to stay at the same weight
60 x 111 = 6660 kilojoules
This lady is fairly active so we add in 20% = 7992 Round this off to 8000 kilojoules
This means given her current lifestyle if she eats 8000 kilojoules of food per day she will remain at 60 kg. If over time she averages less she should lose weight

She would like to be 55 Kg.
55 x 111 = 6105 kilojoules (1450 Calories)
add 20% = 7326 rounded out 7300 kilojoules (1740 calories)
If she now eats at an average of 7300 kilojoules she will have a deficit of 700 kilojoules per day.

How quickly should I lose weight?

700 kilojoules (166 Calories) difference in her diet will not even be noticed.

If for instance she has 1 soda pop and a bar of chocolate a day this would make up this number of kilojoules.

1 gram of fat stores 9 Kilocalories or 37.8 Kilojoules . This represents 18.5 grams of fat which she should lose per day.

Doing this will take her 270 days or 9 months to lose her weight and stabilise.

This sounds an awfully long time .

There again if she actively started to watch what she ate and stuck to a 5000 kilojoule diet i.e. 3000 kilojoules less than she needs to stay at her current weight she should lose 80g per day or 560g kg per week

3000 Kj less per day — she should lose 80 g per day or
560 g per week.

If she then stuck to this amount of energy/food intake she could expect to achieve a weight of 55Kg after 63 days. {That is 5000 divided by 80}. This translates into 9 weeks as opposed to 9 months.

Note the figures below.

$$1000g = 9000 \text{ Kilocalories (Calories)} = 37800 \text{ Kilojoules}$$

$$1Kg = 2.2 \text{ pounds} = 35. 2 \text{ oz}$$

The bottom line is that the speed at which you lose weight depends upon how much you limit the intake.

This program will give you the tools and the method to structure your weight loss according to your aims.

You decide how quickly and how feasible it is to lose the weight.

CONTENTS:

Week One

ACTION!

FIRST TASK
>1.   Assess your current health status

In order to assess the degree of improvement after instituting the program and record your triumph over the bulge, we need to know what you are like before we start.   Thus we need some baseline measurements.
Equipment required:
- Scale or access to scale
- Tape measure

Record the following:
The measurements marked with an asterisk are "nice-to-have" but not essential.

An explanation of how to perform the measurements follows.

CURRENT HEALTH STATUS   Date:

Height	
Weight	
Circumference of Arm	
Circumference of Chest	
Circumference of Abdomen	
Circumference of Hips	
Blood Pressure	
Resting Pulse Rate	
Pulse Rate after 10 Knee Bends	
Pulse Rate after 20 Knee Bends *	
Fasting Blood Sugar *	
Fasting Total Cholesterol *	
Fasting HDL Cholesterol *	
Fasting LDL Cholesterol *	
Fasting Triglycerides *	
Time of PRE of "somewhat hard" Exertion	

- **WEIGHT**

Weigh yourself.

Use the same scale every time you weigh yourself. The best will be a balance scale as spring scales are notoriously inaccurate. More important however, is to **use the same scale**. We are going to judge your progress according to your initial weight. Thus to obtain a fair assessment you must use the same scale each time.

- We do not think it necessary to weigh yourself too frequently so even if you do not have a scale it is not that important. Your local pharmacy will have one or even your local railway station or even a friend. Make use of a scale that you can access easily and ensure that it will be the same one each time. Weigh yourself in the same state each time. It would be best to weigh yourself naked but as long as you weigh yourself in the same attire it makes no difference.

Obviously if you weigh yourself the first week and you are wearing army boots and a winter coat, you cannot compare this to your weight in a bikini costume. Comparisons must be accurate to be valid.

BODY MEASUREMENTS
Perform the following measurements and record them:
- Circumference of upper arm
- Circumference of thigh
- Circumference of hips
- Circumference of abdomen
- Circumference of chest

All of these must be measured at their widest or largest point.
In Ladies either measure above or below the breasts. Record this and always repeat the same measurement.

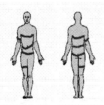
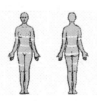

RESTING PULSE
Measure your pulse rate when resting i.e. that is the number of heartbeats over one minute. The most accurate resting pulse is taking your pulse on awakening- still in bed and before your

morning tea or coffee.

You can measure this at your wrist (radial pulse), in your neck (carotid pulse) or directly over your heart.

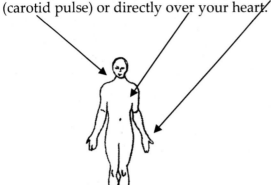

Pulse Rate following 10 knee bends

If you cannot do this accurately or are not sure, ask a friendly health care worker to show you how, or do it for you.

NB!! NB!! NB!!!

Do not perform this exercise if:

1.   You have any known cardiac/heart problem
2.   You have any condition of the knees that precludes you from bending
3.   You have a resting heart rate of 100 or more.

Knee bends are performed by standing with your legs apart and bending at the knee until you are on your haunches. Then stand up so that you are erect again. Do this as fast as you can. Measure your pulse rate before starting and immediately after performing 10 knee bends.

Stop performing this exercise if you become excessively tired or experience any untoward discomfort. Record your pulse rate and number of knee bends performed at this point.

Pulse rate following 20 knee bends

This is as above but obviously doing 20 of the same knee bends. The same precautions apply. Only do this if you are able to.

Fasting blood sugar, cholesterol and triglycerides

These investigations are usually performed on the advice or instigation of your medical practitioner. You can explain to your practitioner that you are taking part in this program and want to assess your basic fitness and compare this again at the end of the program.

Exercise to perceived rate of "somewhat hard" exertion.

Rating of perceived exertion

This fancy term means that, if you are exercising, the way you feel is pretty accurate in predicting the intensity of exercise you are performing. One can perform sophisticated tests on heart rate, oxygen uptake or levels of lactate in the blood to determine how hard you are exercising. This can only be done with sophisticated equipment and technology. It is not necessary however as it has been found that by listening to your body you can also be aware of how hard you are exercising. In other words, if you feel that the exercise is light, it probably is, and not placing too much stress on your body.

However, if you feel that whatever you do is "somewhat hard" or "very, very hard" then it is, and you are stressing your body accordingly.

A rate of perceived exertion that is light is, for instance, walking leisurely. This does not feel difficult and you would be able to talk to a friend whilst walking without any difficulty.

If you exercised or walked at a rate of perceived exertion of "somewhat hard" you would be walking fairly briskly but still able to converse although you would be breathing fairly heavily. If you were exercising at a rate of "very, very hard" you would be going flat out and be unable to talk as all your effort would be going into maximum exercise.

"Hard" would represent well aware of the effort; that your heart rate and breathing rate have increased and you can only talk with breaths inbetween phrases or sentences.

We want you now to perform some exercise until you reach a rate of perceived exertion of "somewhat hard".

You can choose walking, running, swimming, running upstairs, bicycle riding or any form of exercise you care to perform.

Time how long it takes you to reach a stage where you think the intensity of exercise is "somewhat hard".
As an example we will take walking briskly.
- First of all do a few stretches and walk comfortably for about five minutes
- Stretch again
- Now start timing and begin walking briskly

Choose a course you will be able to repeat at some future time i.e. walk around the block. Walk briskly until you feel you are exercising "somewhat hard".
Measure the distance e.g. 3½ blocks and the time e.g. 6 minutes and 30 seconds.

It does not have to be walking. You could swim pool lengths or walk up some flights of stairs. Whatever exercise you do, do it until you feel you have been exercising "somewhat hard".

Photographs

Need we say more? Just like a TV or magazine ad. Take a "before" so that you can compare with the result later.

Now we have a baseline - this is the "before". At the end of the 10 weeks these will be the measurements we will perform again to assess your improvement.

ACTION!
SECOND TASK

Record the food you eat:
- Start to fill in your Honesty Book
- Record everything that passes your lips
- Keep the book on your person
- Record the amounts as portions

EQUIPMENT :
1.   HONESTY BOOKLET
When you received your package after purchasing the program you will have been sent a book- Beat the Bulge and another book- the Honesty Book

Record all the food you eat every day in this Honesty Book

The exception
Water and liquids that contain less than 1 calorie or 5 kilojoules e.g. Diet cool drinks. Do not worry if you do not know what calories or kilojoules are. You will later on as we get into the program.

Below is an example of your table in the Honesty Book. Details are explained in the following pages.

Date	Day	PD 1	
Time	Food/drink	Portion	Total
Part Portions			

In the title bar of the table:

Day refers to day of the week e.g. Monday

PD = program day. This is a 70 day program (10 weeks) so that PD1 is the first day of the program

Total is an accumulative or running total.

Food/Drink:

Write down exactly what you eat or drink.

Portions and **part portions** are described below.

PORTIONS:

You don't know what that is?

Easy

You have a hand and you know what a coffee cup is.

A portion of a solid is the area of the palm of your hand and a portion of liquid is one coffee cup full.

This is the quantity that you eat or drink.

You need to have **four** measurements to consider.

1. **The palm of your hand**.
   The thickness of the foodstuff must not be greater than the thickness of your index finger

2. **A 240ml coffee cup (8 oz)** ***** Note this size cup
   1 Cup = 240ml or 8 fluid ounces

3. **A tablespoon - 15mls.**

4. **A tennis ball or two golf balls**

A portion of food is:
   - Equivalent to the area of the palm of your hand
   - Or the amount that would fit into a coffee cup
   - Where fats or sauces are concerned a portion is a Tablespoon
   - One fruit the size of a tennis ball or two golf balls constitutes a portion
   - Disregard water or diet drinks that contain less than 1 calorie or 5 kilojoules.

If you are eating out or have had your food dished out, you cannot say "Whoa, we must first just measure what you are giving me as I am on my new diet kick".

If however, you have these concepts as above, you can predict with a fair amount of accuracy what you are eating.

Try it and see.

Is the amount of rice on your plate covering roughly the area of the palm of your hand or one cupful?
How big is the slice of bread?
How much gravy did you add? Two tablespoons will gain you two portion points.
Consider the palm of your hand
Do not include your fingers!

The area we are talking about

Portion thickness

A portion of bread for instance would fit the palm of a hand and be the thickness of the width of your index finger[

Obviously a large basketball player's portion will be much larger than a petite young refined lady. There again, the different amounts of food or energy to feed the different size bodies are also proportional.

The Coffee Cup
Make certain we are both considering the same size cup. Check a cup and make sure it has a volume of 240 ml.
1 Cup = 240ml or 8 fluid ounces.

Tennis ball

Golf Ball   **Tablespoon**

             X2

There you have it!
You can record what you are eating every day and at every meal.
Remember to record every thing you eat or drink– other than water and diet drinks less than 1 calorie or 5 kilojoules.
No cheating!
You have to carry your **Honesty book** with you all the time and have a pen with you. It really is no good to think you can fill it in at the end of the day. We all have selective recall and will forget the portion that counts. Remember how little more than your daily needs you have to eat to gain weight?

Are you really serious? Are you seriously serious?
There is no easy way and don't think you can fool us. We have been there. I once went to an Italian restaurant. Wonderful food, ended up with a few Italian kisses for dessert and some liqueurs. I thought that I probably had a little extra to eat, but the truth of the matter was that when I recorded it, it turned out that I had consumed the equivalent of three day's food in one sitting!!

There is no doubt that I did not consider it any where near that amount of food.

IF YOU DON"T RECORD IT YOU ARE ONLY FOOLING YOURSELF!!

Think again of the reason why you are following this training program. The benefits are for you. You will gain if you follow the program, but if you short-change the system you only are short-changing yourself.

Keep that book and pencil handy. Only when you see what you are doing can we institute changes.

At first it may seem difficult and time consuming but like everything you will soon get used to it and practised in this art of gauging what you are eating. Start it and see. At the end of the week you will be doing just fine.

Part Portions:
This is if you take a bite of someone's piece of cake or sandwich for example. You may also be given a sweet or candy by someone. It may sound ridiculous to write it down but you MUST. Remember four quarters make a whole and it is easy to "forget" the quarter portion that you ate.

Below is an example of a record that has been filled in.

Date 31-8-05	Day Tues		PD 1
Time	**Food/drink**	**Portion**	**Total**
6.30	Coffee	1	1
7.00	Cornflakes with milk	2	3
	Banana	1	4
9am	Tea	1	5
11am	Tea and biscuit	2	7
12	Doughnut	1	8
1.05pm	Lasagna	2	10
	Bread	2	12
	Butter	1	13
	Coffee	1	14
	Salad	1	15
3 pm	Tea	1	16
	Ice cream	1	17
Part Portions			
12	½ cream doughnut	1/2	
	Red sweet	1/2	
			18

It is better to keep a running total for each page and insert this in the blocked cell at the bottom of the page. It just makes it easier to record at the end of the week.

Also don't stress if you are not too sure whether you should have two portions for lasagna- one for the pasta and one for the meat or is it just one?

As long as you are consistent it does not matter. As time goes by we will record more accurately.

Record everything that passes your lips except water and diet drinks. Do this for the whole week then review what you have done at the end of the week.

Review of Week 1.

From your Honesty Book fill in the following weekly review:

Review: Week 1

Pr Day	Number of Portions	Acc Total
1		
2		
3		
4		
5		
6		
7		
TOTAL		

Total Number of portions for the week =
Average Number of portions per day   =
Weight at the end of the week   =
Weight at the beginning of the week =

What has happened to your weight?

Three possibilities exist:
1.   You have gained weight
2.   Your weight has stayed the same
3.   You have lost weight.

1. <u>You have gained weight</u>

DO NOT LOSE HEART!

The positives about this are:

- That you obviously have been scrupulously honest in your recording. This is crucial and the basis of insights in to why you are putting on weight-
- That you now have a handle on how much you are eating.

What this tells us is that the number of portions you are eating per week is more than your body needs. You are taking in excess food and storing it as fat.

DON'T BE DESPONDENT!!

The solution:

You need to eat less and the way to do this is by reducing your intake by 10%.

We choose 10% to make it relatively easy as you should not end up too hungry if you fool the bod into eating less. This is also training. Your body will adapt to the lesser amounts and eventually make it uncomfortable to eat amounts you previously ate.

Do this (by eating 10% less).

Divide your total weekly amount of portions by 10 and subtract this amount from your total weekly portion – this should be your aim.

For example:

If you ate 140 portions in a week

$1/10^{th}$ of this is 140/10 =14.

140 – 14 = 126 portions in a week or eighteen portions a day.

At 140 portions per week you were averaging 20 portions per day.

Now we are asking you to only cut out 2 portions per day – this is manageable.

GO TO IT!

2. <u>Your weight has stayed the same.</u>

You now have recorded what you eat in a week and this amount provides you with enough energy to keep your weight stable. This is not what you want so we must reduce this intake so that you take in less than your body needs to keep your weight at this level. If you take in less that your body requires, it must dip into its reserves of energy – this is the stored fat and if you start to use this up or burn it off **– you will lose weight.**

Solution

You need to eat less and the way to do this is by reducing your intake by 10%. This is discussed in the previous section.

3. <u>You have lost weight!</u>

Fantastic! Just by being aware of what you have eaten, you have lost weight.

This weight loss lark should be a doddle if you have done this well! How difficult was it?

If it was a bit of a struggle, stay on the same amount of portions per week and we will review it once again at the end of this next week. If it was no problem, then let us move to the next step and cut your intake by 10%.

Once again the detail of how to do it is discussed on the previous page.

Now decide upon how many portions per day you will aim for in the next week.

Remember: The rate of weight loss depends upon the targets you set yourself refer to page 90.

Week Two

ACTION!

HERE WE GO AGAIN

This week's tasks are to:
1. Implement the eating of your planned number of portions.
2. Record in your honesty book all that passes your lips but try to classify the food into Food Groups.
3. Make a relaxation/hypnosis tape to help you stick to your program.

1. At the end of last week, you calculated the number of portions per day and per week that you planned to eat – insert this in your honesty Book and stick to the plan.

Food groups are as follows:

We will follow the scheme as set out in the Food Pyramid. This is found on the next page. The Food Pyramid is discussed in more detail on pages 25 – 32.

The Food Pyramid - recommended portions

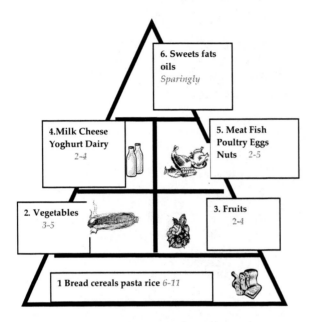

This is the basic food pyramid and represents the mix of foods you should try to eat – more on the bottom and fewer from the top! This pyramid will appear in your Honesty Book for quick reference so you are not expected to remember them. The figures in grey are the recommended number of portions you should try to eat per day. This represents a balanced healthy diet and is recommended by most dieticians and national experts. It is good for you to try and classify the foods you eat to see if you are eating a healthy balanced diet and where you can improve matters.

The following is an example of the Honesty Book you will fill in for this week.

Date	Day		PT		PD 11
Time	Food /Drink		Gp	Por	Tot
Gp	1	2	3	4	5	6	U	Tot

PT is Portion Target. This is the number of portions you plan to eat per day.

PD is program day. The first day of the second week is the 8th day of your program

Gp is Food Group

Por is number of portions – include part portions

Tot is the accumulative total.

On the bottom of the table are the groups listed again

Gp	1	2	3	4	5	6	U	Tot

This is to help you count them daily and at the end of the week. As you record your food and fill up the first page you can summarise it by entering the information below.

The groups are as summarised in the Food Pyramid. The **U** stands for uncertain and if you do not know which food group your food is assigned to just record it as uncertain.

Here follows an example.

Date 22-1-05	Day Sun			PT 24		PD 11	
Time	Food /Drink				Gp	Por	Tot
0800	Coffee				U	1	1
	Cornflakes&milk				1,4	2	3
	Bread 2 slices				1	2	5
	Butter				4	1	6
	Honey				6	1	7
1100	apple				3	1	8
	Tea				U	1	9
1300	Bread 4 slices				1	4	13
	butter				4	2	15
	cheese				4	2	17
	lettuce				2	1	18
1500	Coca cola				6	1	19
1700	beer				U	2	21
	peanuts				5	2	23
	Chips				6	½	23½
							23½
Gp	1	2	3	4	5	6	U	Tot
	7	1	1	6	2	2½	4	23½

Here you will see I was uncertain as to where coffee fitted in so I recorded it as U= uncertain.

The second entry, where I had cornflakes with milk for breakfast, could be recorded as I have done it. It could also have been recorded as one portion in the uncertain group or even two on separate lines to make it easier for yourself.

The two totals at the bottom of the page should be equal.

This also gives you some idea about the composition of your diet.

Does yours fit into the recommendations for a well balanced diet?

Each day is similar and to help you stick to this recording we want you to make an hypnosis tape. The theory about hypnosis can be found in the main section of the book if you have any doubts about it. (Pages 33-46.)

What follows are the instructions about how to make this tape.

Making your Hypnosis Tape

Use this to motivate yourself and to help you maintain and persist with your new eating plan.

The theory and reasoning are not presented here. This can be found on pages 33-46.

You Need:
1. **A tape recorder able to record your voice and replay it.**
2. **Tape with 10-15 minutes clear recording time.**

Record the following "patter".

Read with a calm and clear voice, a little slower than normal communication speech.

This is what you will listen to once you have taped it.

The Hypnotic Patter {Read the following aloud and record it on a tape}

"This tape is being made to help with your new healthy lifestyle.
Find a time of the day when you will not be disturbed.

Lie down on a comfortable couch or bed with your clothing loosened so that you are comfortable and with your legs uncrossed.

Instructions Week 2

Fold your hands across your tummy with your fingers clasped together loosely and comfortably.

Start breathing slowly in and out and concentrate on relaxing and feeling comfortable.

If for any reason, you should be disturbed whilst listening to this tape, you will be able to wake immediately, be alert and attend to whatever it is that has disturbed you.

If this occurs, turn off the tape and when a more opportune moment presents itself, return, rewind your tape and begin again.

Now close your eyes and concentrate on your breathing.
Breathe slowly in and out - and as you breathe out,....... feel yourself relax ...

Feel all the tension go out of your muscles and feel yourself relaxing, feeling calm and all the while experiencing a sense of tranquility, of well-being easing into your body as you breathe slowly in and out.

Concentrate now on your head and feel it getting heavier and heavier, snuggling into the pillow or cushion, getting heavier and heavier.

Feel those neck muscles relax. Feel all the tension ease out of those taut muscles and feel them soften and relax.

Think of your forehead and feel those taut, tense, wrinkly muscles relax. Feel the contraction around your eyes and nose and your eyebrows relax. Feel your tense jaw muscles relax and feel your teeth stop clenching and the tension flow from your facial muscles. Feel your neck relax and the top of your chest and back do so also.

Feel your entire body, trunk, abdomen, legs and arms relax and all the tension drift away and leave you with a pleasant relaxed drowsy feeling.

As you breathe slowly in and out, you experience a wonderful sense of calm overtake you, a tranquil sense of well-being flooding through your entire body and you feel heavy, drowsy, calm and at peace.

Now we are going to count slowly from one to ten.
All the while you will breathe slowly in and out and with each successive count you will go deeper and sounder asleep. On the count of ten you will be deeply and soundly asleep with every muscle, every cell, every fibre in your body relaxed and only your mind concentrating intently on what we say. Each count will relax you even more and allow you to feel better, calmer, heavy, lethargic, relaxed.

One ....
Think of your head - how heavy but comfortable it feels in the pillow. Think of your neck – the muscles feel relaxed, soft, comfortable and loose. Your facial muscles are relaxed. No tense areas around your eyes, nose, mouth and jaw. You can imagine your face calm, unlined; relaxed ….. A pleasant heavy feeling of drowsiness pervades your entire body.
Think of your body. It feels heavy and comfortable – Your chest and back and abdomen, thighs, calves, feet, shoulders, arms and hands getting heavier and heavier with each breath. But all the while it is a pleasant, heavy, lethargic feeling that feels calm and tranquil.

Two.........
A wonderful sense of well being floods your entire body and you feel peaceful, calm, tranquil, relaxed. With each breath you feel yourself going deeper and sounder asleep. Drifting off into a comfortable, calm world of peace and tranquility. A wonderful respite from every day stresses and you feel yourself sinking deeper

and deeper into this calm, wonderful world of well-being.

Three ……..
Deeper and sounder asleep. Very comfortable, very pleasant, very relaxed, heavier and heavier. Sleepy, tired, relaxed. Every muscle, every fibre, every sinew relaxing, getting heavier and heavier. Comfortable, calm and peaceful. Deep dark sound sleep. Deep, dark, sound sleep. Deep,….. dark,…… sound sleep.

Four …….
Once again think of your head – how heavy but comfortable it feels in the pillow.
Think of your neck. The muscles feel relaxed, soft, comfortable, and pliant. Your facial muscles are relaxed. No tense areas around your eyes, nose, mouth and jaw. You can imagine your face calm unlined; relaxed …… a pleasant heavy feeling of drowsiness pervades your entire body. Think of your body. It feels heavy and comfortable.

Your chest and back and abdomen, thighs, calves, feet, shoulders, arms and hands getting heavier and heavier with each breath. But all the while it is a pleasant heavy lethargic feeling that feels good, calm and tranquil.

Five …….
Now think of your breathing.
Concentrate on your breathing in …. and your breathing out. You will notice that you are breathing more slowly now. This is good because when you relax your entire metabolism slows and you need less oxygen as all your muscles are relaxed. Your whole being feels quiet, calm, tranquil, peaceful, relaxed, comfortable, heavy, pleasant. A wonderful sense of well-being, of total peace and calm spreads through your entire body.

Six .....

Think of your body. It feels heavy, leaden, tired, drowsy, lethargic. Each slow breath takes you deeper and deeper into a dark comfortable world of rest and peace and tranquility. Heavy, tired, calm, deeper and deeper asleep with every muscle, every cell every fibre relaxed and at peace. Very pleasant, very calm, very tranquil.

Seven .....

Concentrate once again now on your head and feel it getting heavier and heavier, snuggling into the pillow or cushion, getting heavier and heavier. Feel those neck muscles now completely relaxed. Notice that all the tension has eased out of those taut muscles and they feel soft and relaxed.

Think of your forehead. There are no more taut, tense wrinkle muscles. Your eyes and nose and eyebrows are relaxed. Your jaw muscles are slack and comfortable. Your teeth are not clenched and a wonderful heavy, lethargic feeling fills your entire body.
Heavy, pleasant, tired, sleepy.
Deep, dark, comfortable sleep.
Deep dark, comfortable sleep.
Your facial muscles feel soft, relaxed and smooth. Your neck is relaxed, as is the top of your chest and back. Feel that your entire body, trunk, abdomen, legs and arms are heavy and comfortable. Your entire body feels heavy, leaden not wanting to be moved from this comfortable, calm, heavy cocoon. As you breathe slowly in and out you experience a wonderful sense of calm, tranquil, well-being flooding through your entire body and you feel heavy drowsy calm and at peace. Heavy, drowsy, deeper and deeper. Pleasant, calm, tranquil.

Eight .....

Heavier and heavier. Deeper and deeper. Calm, tired, pleasant, relaxed. With each successive count and with each successive breath feel yourself drifting ever deeper to that perfect, calm, tranquil world of heavy, tired, pleasant well-being.

You feel calm ... serene ...., relaxed........, heavy........., tired .... lethargic but pleasantly at ease. Every muscle, every cell, every fibre in your body relaxed. .... Only your mind concentrating on what we say.

Nine ....
Heavy ...., tired ...., relaxed ...., lethargic. Think of your toes and legs and feet. They feel heavy, leaden, pressing into the couch. Your thighs and your trunk, your chest your arms .... Heavy, leaden... , total relaxation. Your neck muscles are lax, relaxed. Feel your jaw is slack, ... Your facial muscles relaxed, ... your head heavy in the pillow, your breathing slow and regular. You feel completely at ease ...., calm......., tranquil ....., peaceful ......,Serene ...., a wonderful sense of well-being ... every muscle every cell , every fibre in your body relaxed and at ....

TEN........
You are deeply and soundly asleep. Only your mind is concentrating intently on what we say while the rest of your body is at ease, peace, deep, deep, deep, dark, comfortable sound sleep. Nothing strange, nothing different – just this wonderful sense of total relaxation, of recharging your batteries, of giving your body a complete rest ..... Only your mind sharp and alert, concentrating on what we say,.... focused so that whatever we say will sink into your subconscious like a sponge soaking up water.

Now, you must focus your attention upon your hands, which are clasped together across your tummy.

Once again we are going to count .... Slowly ....

This time we will count up to five.
With each successive count we want you to grasp the fingers of the
opposite hand tighter and tighter, clasping the fingers of the
opposite hand tighter and tighter, clasping the fingers together so
that at the count of five your fingers will be locked up so tightly
together that you will be unable to pull them apart.

One .....
Feel your fingers grip the back of the opposite hand and clasp the
hands together tightly. You will feel pressure but no pain as the
hands and fingers grip each other tighter and tighter together,
locking up so that they are unable to be pulled apart.

Two.....
Your fingers are stuck tightly together as if with super glue. There is
no pain but your hands and fingers continue to grip tighter and
tighter, all the while locking your hands together.

Three ...
You can feel the strain in your forearm muscles, in your fingers, in
your hands as all the while your hands grip tighter and tighter
together. No pain .... Only pressure as those hands lock up, tighten,
stuck together.

Four ....
Your hands are locked up tightly together now. Locked up as if in
the jaws of a vice. No pain, only the intense pressure increasing all
the while ... locking those hands together. Your forearm muscles,
your fingers and hands are beginning to tire now with the strain of
gripping the opposite hand together.

Five ...
Your hands are locked so tightly together they are unable to be
pulled apart. You can feel this incredible pressure but there is no

pain. Your hands are locked up, the muscles tired and weary from the effort of squeezing the hands tighter and tighter together.

Now we want you to try and pull your hands apart but as you do so your hands will grip even tighter and tighter together and you are unable to pull your hands apart. Now you begin to feel your fingers and wrists and hands, and forearms getting tired from trying to pull your hands apart. Even your elbows and upper arms, shoulders and neck begin to feel tense with the effort of trying to pull your hands apart. They are becoming so weary now that you want to relax. So we want you now to relax.

Relax ....
Relax - your fingers … your forearm muscles …. Your elbow … Your upper arm… your shoulders … your neck. Feel the tension drain out of all the muscles as your fingers slip out of their grip and relax once again on your abdomen. You feel this wave of relaxation as a tingle that moves from your fingers to your wrists, … your forearm muscles, … your elbow, … your upper arm, … your shoulders,… your neck, … down into your chest, … your abdomen,… your thighs, … your knees, … your calves, your feet … down to the tips of your toes and you feel yourself drifting even deeper and sounder asleep.

It is in this state of relaxation where everything is calm and comfortable and relaxed, that we can communicate with your subconscious mind and leave suggestions that will stay with you when you are awake.

You will never allow yourself to be hypnotised for any other purpose other than a medical or a dental reason.

Each time you listen to this tape, you will go to sleep; deeper, quicker, and sounder. Each time the message we leave with you will be underlined more firmly in your subconscious mind so that it becomes part of your waking life.

When you wake from here, it will be as though you have been asleep for a long time but you will wake with a calm self-confidence that you are able to handle your new healthy lifestyle much more easily. You will find that you will be able to stick to your proposed eating plan and that you will find the food you plan to eat satisfying, nourishing and filling.

You will be motivated to fill in your honesty book every day and listen to this tape every day. As each day, each minute, each hour passes by that you stick to your new eating pattern you will feel more motivated and confident to continue in this way.

You will eat at least three sensible meals a day and not have the desire to snack and eat in between meals. High calorie foods, junk foods, sweets and all the bad things that you know put on weight will lose their attraction and their hold over you. As the days go by you will feel physically and mentally better and each time you listen to this tape you will find it easier to stick to your healthy lifestyle and achieve the aims you set yourself.

Now we will wake you up by once again counting slowly from one to five.
With each successive count, you will become lighter in your sleep until on the count of five you will open your eyes and be wide-awake. You will feel refreshed as though your batteries have been recharged and feel positive and motivated to continue with your healthy lifestyle.

ONE ...
Feel yourself stirring from a deep sleep. Feel life coming back to those lazy lethargic muscles.

TWO...
Lighter and lighter in your sleep. Becoming more aware of your surroundings, feeling very positive, determined, and certain that you will continue with your new healthy lifestyle.

THREE...
Lighter and lighter in your sleep. Feeling calm, relaxed, with a wonderful sense of well-being, determined, positive, motivated. No desire to snack in between meals, a great need to listen to this tape every day. Fill in your honesty book and feeling very positive as each day brings success in your plan.

FOUR ...
Lighter and lighter in your sleep. You feel yourself coming awake, more aware of your surroundings, positive, determined, motivated. Lighter and lighter in your sleep.

And on the count of **FIVE** you open your eyes and you are awake".

<END OF TAPE>

So there it is.
You have just completed your tape for your self–hypnosis session. When you are ready to partake in this, rewind your tape and at a convenient time and listen to what you have recorded. The secret is to focus on the words and try and concentrate on what you hear.

Listen to the words, do and feel what they tell you and you will reap the benefits.

Find a time when you will not be disturbed for about 15 minutes and then lie down on a couch and listen to the tape.

Instructions Week 2

Remember each time you do this it should become easier and have more effect. This should both help with motivation as well as invoking the relaxation response. The more you use this, the more effective it becomes. Try to use it daily in the beginning to keep you on the straight and narrow and at least weekly thereafter.

As the weeks go by you may find you need help with a particular problem. This may be, for example, that they provide you with a sweet sticky snack at work when they bring you tea. You can easily change the message that you leave yourself on your hypnosis tape to make it easier for yourself. This is your tape with your voice and your input. Use it in any way you want.

GO FOR IT!!

Now that you are ready for the week, you have to record everything that passes your lips once again.

Review Week 2:
At the end of the week, this will be your summary.

Week 2 Summary

Pyramid food groups			
Group	Total portions per week	Av portions per day	Reccom portions per day
1			6-11
2			2-4
3			3-5
4			2-4
5			2-5
6			sparingly
U			
Total			

Instructions Week 2

You will take your daily totals from your records and work out what your daily averages per group are.

You can now compare it with the recommendations that are generally made as to the optimal intake.
The next table will be a summary of the number of portions consumed during the week.

Pr day	No of portions	Acc total	Average portions
8			
9			
10			
11			
12			
13			
14			
Total			

If you fill in this table every day, you can keep a beady eye out on the number of portions you are ingesting every day. This can be a motivation to stick with your portion target.

Now you must work out the average number of portions per day

Average number of
portions per day   =

Weight at beginning of week =

Weight at the end of the week =

What has happened to your weight?

126

This is a repeat of the end of the instructions for week 1. They are repeated as this is the standard management for addressing the weight issue at the end of each week.

Three possibilities exist:

1. You have gained weight.
2. Your weight has stayed the same.
3. You have lost weight.

1. **You have gained weight.**

Do not lose heart.

The positives about this are:

- That you obviously have been scrupulously honest in your recording. This is crucial and the basis of insights in to why you are putting on weight-
- That we now have a handle on how much you are eating.

What this tells us is that the number of portions you are eating per week is more than your body needs. You are taking in excess food and storing it as fat.

Solution:

You need to eat less and the way to do this is by reducing your intake by 10%.

We choose 10% to make it relatively easy as you should not end up too hungry if you fool the bod into eating less. This is also training. Your body will adapt to the lesser amounts and eventually make it uncomfortable to eat amounts you previously ate.

Do this (by eating 10% less).

Divide your total weekly amount of portions by 10 - and subtract this amount from your total weekly portion - this should be your aim.

For example: If you ate 168 portions in a week, 1/10th of this is
168/10 = 16.8 Round off to 17
168-17 = 151 portions in a week or 23 portions a day.
At 168 portions per week you were averaging 24 portions per
day. Now we are asking you to only cut out 1 portion per day -
this is manageable.

2. Your weight has stayed the same.
You now have recorded what you eat in a week and this amount
provides you with enough energy to keep your weight stable. This
is not what you want so we must reduce this intake so that you take
in less than your body needs to keep your weight at this level. If you
take in less than your body requires it must dip into its reserve of
energy - this is the stored fat and if you start to use this up or burn it
off - you will lose weight.

Solution
You need to eat less and the way to do this is by reducing your
intake by 10%. This is discussed on the previous page.

3. You have lost weight!
Fantastic! Just by being aware of what you have eaten means you
have lost weight.
This weight loss lark should be a doddle if you have done this well!
How difficult was it?
If it was a bit of a struggle, stay on the same number of portions per
week and we will review it once again at the end of this next week.
If it was no problem then let us move to the next step and cut your
intake by 10%.
Once again the detail of how to do it is discussed above.

And so—on to Week three! Remember to listen to your tape
regularly. Aim for health! It is your most important asset!

Week 3

Your tasks for this week are the following:

- Calculate your daily portion target
- Eat in the correct portions as per the Food Pyramid
- **Record your exercise**
- Use your Hypnosis tape daily

This week is the same as week 2 with the added task of recording any exercise you take.

Record your intake as before.
Set your daily portion target and try to eat in the proportions as recommended in the Food Pyramid.
The first two pages of each day are as in the 2nd week. The only difference is on the third page of each day.
This is where you record your exercise and the relevant section looks like this.

Exercise performed for the day		
Exercise	**PRE**	**Mins**
Total time exercising		

Remember our aim is to ensure that you are a healthy happy individual. The elixir of youth is exercise and the only foil to the ravages of time.

Exercise: -describe the form of exercise e.g. walking, running, swimming tennis etc.
Mins The number of minutes of exercise

PRE = perceived rate of exertion.

This is Light = L, medium = M or Heavy = H

How hard is heavy and how hard is light? These have been worked out for percentages of your maximum heart rate, VO2 max, lactate level and other fancy sounding parameters but listening to your body is accurate enough for our purposes. If you think it is light exercise it is. If you think it is heavy it is. This will vary from person to person and also depend upon your fitness level.

If you can speak freely and easily whilst carrying out the exercise, it is light. If you puff and blow but can still carry out a reasonable conversation, this is medium intensity exercise. If you cannot talk without forcibly concentrating and breathing heavily, this is heavy exercise.

An example:

Exercise performed for the day		
Exercise	PRE	Mins
Walking	L	30
Tennis	M	75
Total time exercising		105

The big thing with exercise is to *start low and go slow.* There is no exercise that is not beneficial and any exercise is better than none at all. Do not overdo it in the beginning and choose something that you enjoy.

Recording this is to get you into the habit of doing so. We will explain later how it fits in with the energy equation i.e. how it helps in losing weight.

Fill in your honesty book daily and try to keep your summaries up to date on a daily basis as this makes it much easier and takes less time at the end of the week when you review the week.

The last page of week is the summary of your endeavours.
As regards exercise for this week and the summary you only have to fill in the number of minutes completed each day. Disregard the PRE for the summary.

Week 3 Summary

Food Pyramid groups			
Group	Total portions per week	Av portions per day	Reccom portions per day
1			6-11
2			2-4
3			3-5
4			2-4
5			2-5
6			sparingly
U			-
Total			

Program Day	Portions	Total Portions	Mins exercise
15			
16			
17			
18			
19			
20			
21			
Total for week			
Average per day			

Weight at beginning of Week =

Weight at the end of the week =

Once again you have the three possibilities. You have either lost weight, gained weight or stayed the same.
If you have gained weight or stayed at the same weight, your portion target for the next week must be reduced by 10 %.
I f you have lost weight and feel fine, try also reducing by 10% but if it has been a struggle, you can stay at the same portion target.

Write down your **daily portion target for week 4**

Portion target per day for next week

=

Week Four

ACTION!

Here we go again!

This week's tasks are to:
1. Implement the eating of the planned number of portions. At the end of last week you calculated the number of portions per day that you are to aim for this week. Write this down in your portion target and follow the same system as last week.

2. Record in your honesty book all that passes your lips but try to eat in the correct proportions of the Food groups

3. Record the amount of exercise you perform per day

4. **Start to use the concept of calories or kilojoules.**

Calories and Kilojoules (More detailed discussion pg 47-58)
How do we compare pears with apples or ice-cream with lettuce leaves. We all know that if you eat chocolates and ice-cream you will gain more weight than if you eat lettuce leaves and carrots.
The reason is that the chocolate and ice-cream contain more energy than the vegetables.

Our body requires energy or fuel to function. Food provides that energy. If you take in the correct amount of energy for your daily functions, you will be in equilibrium and you will stay at the same weight.

If you use up more energy than you take in you will lose weight because your body will burn or use up your energy reserves.

Energy reserves in the body are stored in fat. If you take in more energy than your body needs it will be converted into and stored as fat.

We need a method of comparing energy values and this is what calories or kilojoules are all about.
Unfortunately, the world has not yet got around to one universally accepted measurement and that is why we mention both of these.

Use whichever you are comfortable with.

The energy values of all foods can and have been worked out. There are also many formulas for working out how much energy you can take in to remain at the same weight

We can work out how much energy you need to take in daily to stay at the same weight.

We can also work out how much energy you are taking on board by recording the amount of calories you take in in food and drink. We can also calculate how many you use up when exercising.

This is what you will be doing this week.

Calculating your portions as Calories or Kilojoules

Calories are more correctly called kilocalories but they are used interchangeably and mean the same thing.

Kilojoules and calories are units of energy that we can use to compare foods. 1 calorie = 4.2 kilojoules.

Each foodstuff has a calorie or kilojoule value. These are just different units. For brevity and ease of reading, I will just talk about

Calories in the next section. If you are more familiar with Kilojoules, do not worry– we have given kilojoule values for you to use. It is merely during the theoretical bit where we only talk about calories.

In your honesty booklet, we have put down values for the different food groups. It looks like this:

Group	Description	Cal	Kj
1 Low	Bread Cereal	100	420
1 High	Pasta Rice	200	840
2 Low	Peas Beans	40	160
2 Med	Broccoli Cabbage	80	320
2 High	Potato boiled mash	100	420
3 Low	Peach apricot orange	50	210
3 High	Apple Pear Banana	100	420
4 Low	Yoghurt cup 240ml	100	420
4 High	Milk/cup Cheese 1 Ts	160	670
5 Low	Fish Egg 10 Nuts	100	420
5 Med	Chicken	215	900
5 High	Beef Lamb	345	1450
6 Low	Salad oil	100	420
6 High	Mayonnaise	130	550
	Fat Cooking oil 1 Ts	155	650
	Chocolate candy 30g		
Drinks	Water diet drinks	0-5	0-20
	Pop alcohol 240 ml	100	420
	Tea coffee black	5	20
Misc	Milk 1 Ts 15 ml	10	40
	Sugar 1 ts 5 ml	20	80
	Uncertain	200	840

The value is what a portion will supply. Obviously, this is a very rough estimate but it is a way of becoming familiar with calorie counting.

This table has the calorie or Kilojoule value of each food group. You will note there is a *high* or a *low* value. Only a representative food has been chosen, so you need to make an educated guess if the food you are eating is not on the list. We will give you lists that are more comprehensive later on. These are to get you into the culture of counting. If the food you are eating is not on the list, estimate which one of the foods in the same group it would most closely approximate and use that value.

If you are still not sure, use the uncertain value.(200cals 840 kj) What do you do about the uncertain portions— The highest portion score is 345 calories (1450 Kj) and the lowest is 0. We compromise by putting it in 200 kilocalories or 840 kilojoules. This may be an overestimation in many cases but it is better to overestimate than underestimate.

Thus you will have set as your target the number of portions you aim to ingest per day. Now we want you to work out how much energy value these portions contain. I.e. how many Calories or Kilojoules these portions provide. If it is difficult just do the best you can. "Guestimate" as best you can. This is all practice for the weeks that come. This is your learning curve for using energy intake. Stick with it. It is not easy but the results -HEALTH– are worth any effort.

Remember this is all part of your training. Knowledge is the power! When you discover which foods are causing your problem and how different foods can make a difference you have the tools to change!

The next table in the honesty booklet is one which indicates how many Calories or Kilojoules are used when exercising.

Energy expended in exercise per minute		Cals Kcals	Kilojoules
Perceived rate of exercise	Light	3	13
	Moderate	5	21
	Heavy	10	42

Thus if for example you go for a brisk walk for 1/2 an hour at a perceived rate of exertion of moderate exercise you would expend

30 x 5 calories = 150 calories or

30 x 21 kilojoules = 630 kilojoules

Once again, it is a rough estimation and Calorie and Kilojoule values will not always correlate 100%

The tables in the honesty book now look like this

Food group   number of portions   Accumulative total of portions

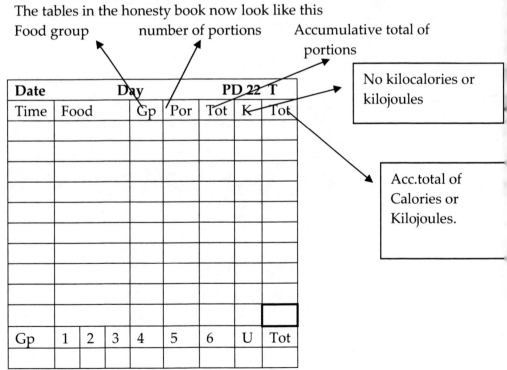

No kilocalories or kilojoules

Acc.total of Calories or Kilojoules.

Date		Day			PD 22 T		
Time	Food		Gp	Por	Tot	K	Tot
Gp	1	2	3	4	5	6	U	Tot

T=Target i.e. the old portion target

Instructions Week 4

These are standard, as you have used before except now you will try to put the food in groups (Gp). Estimate the number of portions (Por) and the first "Tot" refers to the running or accumulative total of your portions.

The K is for the estimated number of Kilocalories (calories) or Kilojoules of the portion. The Tot that follows this is the running or accumulative total of the energy value- Calories (Kilocalories) or Kilojoules.

The third page of each day looks as follows.

Date		Day			PD 25	T	
Time	Food		Gp	Por	Tot	K	Tot

Gp	1	2	3	4	5	6	U	Tot

Time			Exercise			
	Type		PRE		Mins	K

Total energy expenditure	
Total energy intake	
Effective Daily Intake Intake – expenditure	

An example of how it would be filled in follows. What is helpful is if you keep your running or accumulated totals up to date each time you enter any information. This makes it so much easier each evening when you are summarizing the day's intake and expenditure.

Note that at the bottom of page 2 of that particular day 19 portions would have been recorded and the running total of the Kilojoules would have been 4020.

Example

Date	Day				PD 25 T		
Time	Food	Gp	Por	Tot	K		Tot
7pm	Pasta	1	2	21	1680		5600
	Mince	5	1	22	2900		8500
	Gravy	6	1	23	420		8920
	Salad	2	2	25	320		9240
830pm	Coffee	U	1	26	105		9345
							9345

Gp	1	2	3	4	5	6	U	Tot
	2	2			1	1	1	29

Time	Exercise			
	Type	PRE	Mins	K
5pm	Running	L	30	390

Total energy expenditure	390
Total energy intake	9345
Effective Daily Intake	8955
Intake – expenditure	

Fill in each day's information and at the end of the week we will review what you have done.

Review Week 4

Food Pyramid food groups			
Group	Total portions per week	Av portions per day	Reccom portions per day
1			6-11
2			2-4
3			3-5
4			2-4
5			2-5
6			sparingly
U			~
Total			

Total up the number of portions you consumed this week and compare the averages with the recommended for healthy living.

Review of calories or kilojoules ingested and expended

This is your energy balance- the total number of units taken in minus those used up in exercise.

This is what the summary looks like in the honesty book.

Summary of week's energy intake

PD	Effective Daily intake	Acc Total	Daily Average
	Calories or Kilojoules		
22			
23			
24			
25			
26			
27			
28			
Weekly Total			

Fill in your effective daily intake from each day's summary.

Fill in your weight at the beginning and the end of the week.

Week Five

ACTION!

This week's tasks are to:

- Calculate the number of Kilocalories or Kilojoules you need to stay at the same weight.
- Decide what you aim to consume on a daily basis.
- Use your Kilocalorie or Kilojoule counter book.
- Calculate how much energy you dissipate during exercise
- Make sure your tape is helping you.

This week is different in that you are not bringing over any calculations or targets to aim at from last week. The fourth week was to get you used to counting energy units (calories or kilojoules)

Your first task this week is to calculate how many Calories or kilojoules you can ingest to stay at the same weight.

Once you have done this you must then set your target at what you believe is achievable for this week.

Calculate the number of Kilocalories or Kilojoules you need to stay at the same weight.

To stay at the same weight the following calculation will tell you how many Kilojoules or Cals (Kilocalories) you can consume per day. Recalculate this with your current weight.

What is your weight?

Use the units you are comfortable with.

Calories or Kilocalories

Your weight in lbs   X   12   = ... calories

Your weight in Kgs   X   26.4 = ...calories

Kilojoules:

Your weight in lbs   X   50.4 =.........Kilojoules

Your weight in Kg   X   111.0 =.........Kilojoules

Now you must take your weight at the beginning of this week. What it is now and multiply it by the relevant factor to work out your calculated energy intake to stay at the same weight.
This is your basic energy needs and does not consider exercise in the equation. You need more fuel for exercising. Look upon this as your bonus. The energy you use up exercising is a gain in weight loss.

Decide what you aim to consume on a daily basis.

What is your target? Commit yourself!

What do you think you could aim for? Try just reducing by 10% if you are finding it tough going. The longer you stay with a reduced intake the easier it becomes. Remember, you are in training and training your body to get used to less food– the aim is always worth it. You only have one life and health is the most important asset you have. No health means a poorer standard of life. So do not give in– keep going.

Energy Intake Target =

This week you will have an honesty book for week five as well as a **calorie or kilojoule counter book.**

You might have found it difficult to count or assign an energy value to the foods using the portion value table of last week. You will see that the chart for this week and in the future is much easier and user friendly.

Date	Day	PD 29 T	
Time	Food	K	Tot

Each day has two of these tables, which have only two entities in the right columns. K = Energy values– Kilojoules or Calories, whichever you have decided upon. Tot is the accumulative total. The bottom right cell is in bold. If you fill this in every time your page is full makes it much easier to keep track on a daily and weekly basis. The energy value of the food can be obtained from the Food group portions table as you have done last week. These values can also be found in your personal calorie/Kilojoule Counter section of the Honesty Book.

Group	Description	Cal	Kj
1 Low	Bread Cereal	100	420
1 High	Pasta Rice	200	840
2 Low	Peas Beans	40	160
2 Med	Broccoli Cabbage	80	320
2 High	Potato boiled mash	100	420
3 Low	Peach apricot orange	50	210
3 High	Apple Pear Banana	100	420
4 Low	Yoghurt cup 240ml	100	420
4 High	Milk/cup Cheese 1 Ts	160	670
5 Low	Fish Egg 10 Nuts	100	420
5 Med	Chicken	215	900
5 High	Beef Lamb	345	1450
6 Low	Salad oil	100	420
6 High	Mayonnaise	130	550
	Fat Cooking oil 1 Ts	155	650
	Chocolate candy 30g		
Drinks	Water diet drinks	0-5	0-20
	Pop alcohol 240 ml	100	420
	Tea coffee black	5	20
Misc	Milk 1 Ts 15 ml	10	40
	Sugar 1 ts 5 ml	20	80
	Uncertain	200	840

In addition this week we are now introducing your own personal **Energy (**Calorie/Kilojoule**) Counter.** This can be found on page 254 - 314 of the honesty Book. This section has a number of foods with their energy values in alphabetical order.

Your own personal **Energy Counter** will form the basis of your own personal eating plan as over time you will record the energy values of food and drink that you commonly use.

What follows is an example of a page in this section of the Honesty Book.

B	Quantity	Kcal	Kj
Beetroot boiled	½ cup	30	126
Biscuits- sweet, plain, marie, boudoir	1	20	84
Biscuits rusks	1	20	84
Biscuits choc	1	290	1218
Brandy	21 ml 1tot	75	315
Brazil nuts	10	100	420
Bread white brown rye	1 slice	100	420
Bread roll	1	100	420
Bread whole wheat	1 slice	62	260
Bread & butter pudding	1 small portion	185	777
Broccoli	½ cup	15	63
Brussel sprouts boiled	½ cup	20	84
Butter	1 tsp	55	230
Butter marg	thinly spread	20	84
Butter	120g 4oz	813	3414

Values are given for both Calories and Kilojoules.
NB careful note must be taken of the quantities and the energy value assigned to them. You should be able to estimate the value fairly accurately by using your usual assessment of portions.– Palm of hand, 240 ml cup etc. and comparing the quantity to that recorded in the table.

As you soon will realise, not all foods you eat are documented in your book. Now we want you to customise the book for yourself. Find out the value of the foods you usually use and put them in your book.

Most of us tend to eat a fairly standard diet so it is worthwhile working out the energy value of your commonly consumed foods. There are open pages at the back of your energy counter book to accommodate these foods.

If you don't know the value of a food make a "guestimate" of an equivalent food or look in the food group to which it belongs.

If you have access to the internet you can find most foods and their energy equivalents at the following sites. The owners of these sites have given us permission to advise you to look for values there.

> www.calorieking.com
> www.annecollins.com/calories/index.htm

If you cannot find it there, you can also look it up on the internet by going to www.google.com and putting in the search term "calorie value *'food'* where food is the food you do not know. You can do this even if it is an unusual food.

Eg. Pancit* calorie value. Pawpaw calorie value, shawerma calorie value.

For instance even if you did not know how to spell "Pancit" you will still get to a value. I put in "panset calorie value" and google asked me if I did not mean "pancit." Changing it to this and I was taken to

a site that gave me the answer.
pancit is a delicious philipino dish

Likewise pawpaw or papaya or different spellings of the same will bring you to some site that gives you the answer. Is it shawarma shawourma or some other spelling? The vast resources of the net will find you something. If it is a usual food you eat– look it up if you are serious.

 You can also contact us on www.beatthebulge.co.za and we will help you with this or any other query.

Just be careful when using these, as the portion/amount size and quantity are often not standardized.
If you use the sites that are listed in the calorie counter booklet, you should find most of the information you require.

You can always see what the food is made of and set a value for yourself using the food group portion's value.

The Food groups are divided into high or low value per portion for each group with examples of each.

Also put in your standard meals– so that you will not always have to perform a calculation.
For e.g. if you often have a cheese and tomato sandwich for lunch
You can put this in as a standard **Cheese and tomato sandwich**
    2 slices of bread 2X 100 = 200
    Butter or marge spread   = 20
          Cheese = 100
          Tomato   = 20 cals

Thus every time you have a cheese and tomato sandwich you know this is 340 calories.

Another good idea is to put in the value of your 'weaknesses"
i.e. if you love chocolate or crisps for instance it is a good idea to be
aware of the food value in these items
Most of us tend to stick to familiar foods most of the time so it is
worth while finding out what the value of this is. Many foods are
now sold with packaging that tells you the energy value of these
foods, so always make a habit of checking this. You can then add it
to your own calorie counter book.

The third page of each day of week 5 looks as follows:

Date	Day	PD 29	T
Time	**Food**	**K**	**Tot**
Total energy intake per day			
Exercise			
Mins	**Type**	**PRE**	**K**
Total energy used in exercise			
Balance of energy intake			

Calculate your energy intake and your expenditure. The figure you obtain is the one in the bottom R hand corner. You should transfer this to the table that summarises the week's energy balance.

The best is to fill this in daily so it is easy at the end of the week to see where you stand. Another advantage is that you know what your daily target is.
If the daily average exceeds this it is a motivation to get back into line.
Once again we must stress that it is important to record everything and always keep your honesty book on hand. It is the only way of staying on the straight and narrow.

This is the summary and review of the week:

Summary of Week's Energy Intake and Expenditure

PD	Food	Exer-cise	Total	Acc total	Daily Av
29					
30					
31					
32					
33					
34					
35					
Total					

In the **Food** column is the total energy intake for that particular program day.

In the **Exercise** column, record the amount of energy used up n exercising.

The **Total** column is the day's energy balance i.e. Energy intake – expenditure. This is the same as each day's third page bottom right hand corner figure.

The **Acc Total** is the running or accumulated total of energy units and from this, you can work out the daily average to see if you are keeping to your target.

Summary of Week 5

Weight at the beginning of the week=

Weight at the end of the week   =

Energy balance

Average of Kilojoules/Cals per day =

How does this compare to the target you set yourself at the beginning of the week?

What has happened to your weight?

What has happened to your weight?

Three possibilities exist:
    You have gained weight
    Your weight has stayed the same
    You have lost weight.

1. **You have gained weight**

If the average amount of Calories/Kilojoules per day exceeds that which you calculated at the beginning of the week then you have the answer. You must stick to the amount you estimate.
If you have gained weight and eaten the same or less than you calculated, then the energy calculation is incorrect.

The solution:
You need to eat less and the way to do this is by reducing your intake by 10%.
You must reduce your target energy intake by 10%

Your weight has stayed the same.

If the average amount of Calories/Kilojoules per day exceeds that which you calculated at the beginning of the week then you have the answer. You must stick to the amount you estimate.
If you have stayed the same weight and eaten the same amount or less calories/kilojoules than you calculated, then the energy calculation is incorrect.

The solution:
You need to eat less and the way to do this is by reducing your intake by 10%.

You have lost weight!
Fantastic! This weight loss lark should be a doddle if you have done this well!
How difficult was it?
If it was a bit of a struggle, stay on the same amount of energy units calories or Kilojoules- per week and we will review it once again at

the end of this next week. If it was no problem, then let us move to the next step and cut your intake by 10%.

Now decide upon how many Calories or Kilojoules you will aim for per day in the next week.

Target per day for next week =

Your target energy intake will be worked out according to your weight. This week was a hard one getting into the calorie count and we are sure it will become easier each week as you get more used to it.
Make sure your tape is helping you.

Are you using your relaxation/hypnosis tape? Are you using it effectively?

The more you use it the better the effect.

Do you feel a little silly listening to your own voice on a tape? Do you feel a little anxious that someone may see you and think you a little odd?

There is nothing odd about being healthy and you will have the last laugh when you succeed. Just find a private time when you will not be disturbed.

Tailor your tape to your own needs.

Which times do you find the most difficult? Leave a positive suggestion for these times.

Week 6
Tasks

- Record the energy value of your usual foods
- Identify problem areas
- Design a Rescue day for yourself
- Record the energy value of your "weakness foods"

First of all you must work out the amount of kilojoules or Calories you aim to consume a day. Set the target for each day and use your Tape to help you stay at the same weight.

What is your current weight?

To stay at the same weight the following calculation will tell you how many Kilojoules or Cals (Kilocalories) you can consume per day. Recalculate this with your current weight.

Calories or Kilocalories

Your weight in lbs   X   12   = ... calories

Your weight in Kgs   X   26.4   = ...calories

Kilojoules:

Your weight in lbs   X   50.4   = ... Kilojoules

Your weight in Kg   X   111.0 = ... Kilojoules

Weigh yourself now at the beginning of week 6.

Multiply it by the relevant factor to work out your calculated energy intake to stay at the same weight.

If you have lost weight in week 5 then this calculation will be less than last week. How does your calculation compare with the amount of Energy units you calculated at the end of week 5?

What is your target? Commit yourself!

What do you think you could aim for? Try just reducing by 10% if you are finding it tough going. The longer you stay with a reduced intake the easier it becomes. Remember, you are in training and training your body to get used to less food– the aim is always worth it. You only have one life and health is the most important asset you have. No health means a poorer standard of life. So don't give in– keep going.

Do not allow for exercise. Try to stick to your basic energy needs. Yes, you need more fuel for exercising. Look upon this as your bonus. You could only calculate it with your basic needs if you were doing this regularly in any event.

The energy you use up exercising is a gain in weight loss.

Decide what you aim to consume on a daily basis.

What is your daily energy intake target?

The additional changes this week are to identify problem areas

The pages this week are as below. In the unlined area there is place to record the problems you are having. Try to identify the factors that cause you to eat more than you should. For example, these may be finding tasty snacks left over in the refrigerator or always being hungry in mid morning. Then again you may be unable to resist tucking into the chocolates you were given as a thank you present.

These are just examples but write down anything you can think of that is causing you problems.

Date	Day	PD 37 T	
Time	Food	K	Tot
Problems			

The rest of the table is similar to last week.

The third page of each day also has an unlined section. This one however is for you to devise solutions for the problems you have identified. If it is for instance the problem of tasty left overs in the refrigerator, in future you will dispose of them or if this is too wasteful, plan better that you do not have left overs or make sure you give them away when they occur. This may not be a solution for you but is only an example. The bottom line is for you to think about problem areas and develop you own solution.

Date	Day	PD 36 T	
Time	Food	K	Tot
Total Energy intake per day			
Exercise			
Mins	Type	PRE	K
Total Energy used up in exercise			
Balance of energy intake			
Solutions for problems			

An example of my own:

Problems			
Medical reps bring sweets and snacks			

Balance of energy intake	
Solutions for problems	

Receptionists must not let me have them–
Or even gain sight of them. They must
not be left in my "intray" but divided up
amongst the staff.

This has saved me many extra kilojoules!

Another task for this week is:

Record the energy value of your usual foods
Use your Energy Counter (Kilocalorie/ Kilojoule) book and
customise it for your own use. Record on page 302-305 in the
honesty book.
As you will have realised, not all foods you eat are documented in
your book. Now we want you to customise the book for yourself.
Find out the value of the foods you usually use and put them in
your book.
Also put in your standard meals– so that you will not always have
to perform a calculation.
So your task this week is to make a list of foods you commonly eat
that are not in the calorie counter book.
As discussed before, if you use the sites that are listed in the calorie
counter booklet you should find most of the information you
require.
Another alternative is to put in a search engine– e.g. Google -the
item you are looking for and calorie value and you should get what
you are looking for.
The potential is large and this is why we have not put all foods in
the booklet. It is impossible to cater for everyone's tastes. Use the
pages at the back of the calorie counter book. Below is a truncated

example

Your own frequently used foods			
Food	Quantity	Cals	Kj
Rice Krispies &Milk	1C & 1C	290	1220
Yoghurt Almarai	125ml	130	550
Coffee milk F/C	1 cup	35	150
Peanut butter sandwich 2 slices bread butter pb	100 100 20 50	270	1130

If my usual breakfast is Rice Krispies with one cup of full cream milk I know how many calories this represents so is easy to fill in my honesty book.

Likewise I usually drink coffee with full cream milk and no sugar so I know that this is 35 calories of energy.

My standard peanut butter sandwich is worth 270 calories. This is 100 for each slice of bread, 20 for margarine spread and 50 for the peanut butter.

We all tend to eat the same food on a regular basis so if you put down your usual it makes it much easier to record in future. Another benefit is that you may change what you eat by finding out how many calories the food you like contains.

Then again you may find that some of the food you nowadays purchase has the value of the food recorded on the packaging. For instance, I obtained the value of the bread per slice as 100 calories from the calorie counter book as well as the food portion groups I have provided you. It was a pleasant surprise to purchase pre-sliced bread, which said each slice was 33g in weight and had a calorie value of 70. Therefore, it is always valuable checking your values with officially recorded or measured values.

Design a rescue day for yourself
Another new task this week is to design a rescue day for yourself. In the real world, there will always be a day where, however good your intentions are, you will lapse and eat far more than you planned or intended to eat.

The big thing to do is not to get despondent and think, "Ah well, I've blown it there is no point in my recording any further today." This is a mistake. Keep on recording! It does two things. It will stop you having even more than you intended and it gives you a plan for recovery. If, for instance, you aim at 2000 calories per day but lose the plot and eat 3500 Calories per day: you then know you have to make up 1500 calories in the remaining days if you want to stick to your planned amount. You can do this by reducing the mount taken in over the next few days and also increasing your exercise. But it is a good plan to have a **Rescue Day** up your sleeve.

By this we mean a planned day of three low calorie meals that total about 1000 calories/4200 kilojoules. In other words a low calorie value that you are comfortable with and know you can stick to. It is also a good idea to record this in your calorie counter book

It is anything you will be happy with. The more different rescue days you have, the better it will be for you.

For instance, you may have:

Rescue Day 1.—Figures are in Calories unless otherwise stated.

Breakfast.	Rice Krispies 1 Cup	
	Milk Full cream 1 Cup	190 Cals(160 +130)
Lunch:	2 Sandwiches with Jam	270
Snack:	1 Apple	100
Supper	1 Portion Steamed Fish	70
	1 Boiled Potato	100
	Peas 1/2 Cup	35
	Pumpkin	45

All drinks during the day only water or diet drinks
This is a total of   **910 Cals or 3800 kilojoules**

Rescue Day 2.

Breakfast	Corn Flakes—1 cup 30g	120
	Milk low fat 1 cup	85
Lunch	100g of Yoghurt	70
	1 Cup fruit	50
	1 thin bread and marg	105
Supper—vegetarian		
	2 potatoes– boiled 2 X100g	130
	4 courgettes	90
	Pumpkin	45
	Butter 1 Ts	145

All drinks water or diet

This gives a total of   **840 Calories or 3530 Kilojoules**

Put these in as a standard in your Calorie/Kilojoule counter book on page 308-309

Your own frequently used foods			
Food	Quantity	Cals	Kj
Rescue day 1		910	3800
Rescue day 2		840	3530

Record the energy value of your "weakness" foods. On page 306-307

This is another task for this week and also customising your Calorie/kilojoule counter booklet.

We all have weaknesses.

Mine are cheese and ice-cream.

Yours may be chocolates or Kentucky fried Chicken, French fries, cheese cake, doughnuts or cream cakes. The list is endless and there are many tasty temptations out there.

The path to health and fitness is a tough one. But the benefits are immense.

In the same way as you have put your usual foods into your Kilojoule/Calorie Counter bookle, do the same for your weakness foods.

You can also display this list up in strategic places– the refrigerator door, in the cabinet or cupboard where they are kept.

An example is as follows:

Your own frequently used foods			
WEAKNESS or DANGER FOODS!!!!!			
Food	Quantity	Cals	Kj
Ice-cream	1 cup	300	1260
Chips/crisps	30g	150	630
French fries	100g	330	1380
Chocolate	30g	155	650
Peanuts	1cup	800	3360
Cream High fat 50%	1Ts	130	546
Cream 35%	1Ts	65	270
Cheese	30g	120	504

Use all these strategies to help you achieve your goal. Having an occasional relapse is not a reason to give up. Redo your Tape. Make sure you listen to it each day. Use a rescue day! The rewards of good health await you. Keep going!!

Summary of Week's Energy Balance

PD	Food	Exer-cise	Total	Acc total	Daily Av
29					
30					
31					
32					
33					
34					
35					
Total					

Record the daily energy intake in Kilojoules or Calories. Do the same for the expenditure- the exercise. You can even short circuit this by just recording the total each day and the accumulated total. If you divide the accumulated total by the number of days you have been following the program this week, you will be able to know what your daily average is. You can compare this with your target energy intake for the day. If you are falling behind, this will motivate you to slow down on the intake.

Summary of Week 6

Weight at the beginning of the week=

Weight at the end of the week   =

Energy balance

Average of Kilojoules/Cals per day =

Target per day for next week   =

Set this target according to your weight. What do you think you can achieve?

Week 7

Tasks

The extra tasks for this week are to

- Eat only vegetables on one day of the week

- Eat only fruit on one day of the week

This seems a little odd and difficult. The reason why we want you to do this is to see what the benefits are. Fruit and vegetables are low energy foods and contain many vitamins and minerals. They are always mentioned in any healthy eating diet but unfortunately few of us eat the recommended number of portions of these per day.
I want you to use your ingenuity and you will find that it is possible to eat vegetables for breakfast and fruit for supper.
I am sure you will also be impressed with the low number of kilojoules or calories you ingest on these days. It is almost certainly guaranteed to be lower than your calculated same weight energy amount per day. (SWEAD).

For example below are some values of vegetables with low energy values

Low value vegetables	Quantity	Kcal	Kj
Asparagus	6 stalks	15	64
Beans French runner	½ cup	25	105
Broccoli	½ cup	15	63
Brussel sprouts boiled	½ cup	20	84
Cabbage raw	½ cup	28	100
Cabbage boiled	½ cup	20	84

166

You can find values for most fruits and vegetables in either the personal energy counter or by accessing one of the following links:

- **www.annecollins.com**

- **www.calorieking.com**

Whatever combinations you try you should be able to work out an effective low value fruit or vegetable day which could also double as a rescue day.

Remember you are training for life. In the future there will be days when you overindulge and you have to have a strategy for getting back on track. These days of all fruit or all vegetables may be a solution for you.

So, what are the fruits and vegetables you enjoy?

What novel ways can you think of preparing them?

Remember also that if you add in salad dressings to salads or cream to your fruit etc *these are in the Food group 6 — the high calorie foods. They will add to the unwanted calories.* Don't spoil the gains by trying to make the food too tasty!

Over to you and your ingenuity!

Week 8
Tasks

- Work out your **actual** same weight energy balance

- Use all the strategies you have learnt over the past weeks

The easiest is to follow all the strategies you have learnt.

The big task this week is to work out your actual SWEAD

the **S**ame **W**eight **E**nergy **A**llowance for the **D**ay

What do we mean by this?
There are innumerable formulas out there to work out the amount of energy you can ingest to say at the same weight. There is no one recognized formula and all have their supporters and their detractors.

The truth of the matter is that they are only guidelines. We are using them to help. Now is the time to work out more accurately what is correct for you or more accurately, what is closer to your own SWEAD.

You are unique! You are not like a car model with the same parts and characteristics as all similar models. Your thumbprint is unique as is the pattern of your iris– both systems that can be used to identify you as a unique individual. So why should the way you handle food and energy be any different.

Thus this week's task is to come closer to the values that more accurately reflect your own unique physiology.

You will have seen that there are various values for Calorie counts. For example, you will see we have said a slice of bread is worth 100 calories. You may look on the back of the wrapping of a loaf of pre-sliced bread and find a statement "1 slice of bread = 33g = 70 Cals."

Now who is correct? There may even be a different value in books you use or internet sites you access.
The amount of calories to stay at the same weight in our calculations may also be lower than the amount that actually should be allowed to stay at the same weight.
Likewise working out the number of Calories or kilojoules you expend whilst exercising may have been underestimated in our calculations.

It does not really matter. You have to use one set of values that suits you. I deliberately chose higher values to try to ensure you have a better chance of losing weight.

By now, you will have seen if the values you are using have resulted in a weight loss or gain.

If you go to your last page of the last few weeks in your honesty book, you will see that you have an average per day of energy consumed.

You also have either a weight gain or a weight loss.

By now, you will also have an idea of the usual values you use. Thus if you continue to use these values both for energy intake i.e. food and energy expenditure i.e. exercise you will get an idea of the amount of calories you should aim at to stay at the same weight.

So, if for instance, you started the week at 78 Kg and worked out, using our formula and the values in our books, that to stay at the same weight you could have 78 x 26.4 = 2059 calories. At the end of the week, your weight is 77.5 Kg.

So how many Cals did you use up? You work out your energy balance to be 1977 calories per day. That is your average energy intake - (minus) your energy expenditure (exercise) per day.

You lost 0.5 Kg. Therefore, your amount allowed to stay at the same weight is higher than the 1977 Cals per day that you worked out and may even be the 2059 that you calculated as your same weight target. Thus using these figures- even if they would not allow you to win a prize for scientific accuracy- will still help you set a realistic target for weight control.

If your calculations mirror these, i.e. you have lost weight, then you can use these same figures and portions to continue, but your proper SWEAD is greater than this number.

If you find you are gaining weight with your calculated amounts, then you have to cut the amount.

Once again, do so by 10 % until you find the amount that says this is the amount of calories that will keep you at the same weight. Then you have a figure to aim at and aim to eat less than that amount in order to lose weight.

Consider that you lost 0.5 Kg over the week.

You did this by ingesting an average of 1977 calories per day

0.5 Kg = 500 grams

Theoretically I gm of fat stores 9 Calories of energy

500 = 4500 Cals over 7 days = 643 Cals per day

1977 + 643 = 2620

Thus, perhaps 2620 calories is the daily energy value you should be allowed to ingest to stay at the same weight. Anything below that and you will lose weight.

Similarly, what if you have gained weight? For example if you had gained 0.5 Kg you have taken in an extra 4500 Cals over the week and need to reduce your intake by 643 Cals per day to stay at the same weight.

Let us look at the latest calculations from the World Health Organisation (WHO):

Revised WHO Equations for Estimating Energy Expenditure

> **Total energy expenditure = basal metabolic rate x activity factor**

Estimate basal metabolic rate

Men:
18-30 years = (0.0630 x actual weight in Kg + 2.8957) x 240 kcal/day

31-60 years = (0.0484 x actual weight in Kg + 3.6534) x 240kcal/day
Use the second equation if you are older than 60 years

Women :
18-30 years = (0.0621 x actual weight in Kg + 2.0357) x 240 kcal/day

31- 60 years = (0.0342 x actual weight in Kg + 3.5377) x 240 kcal/day

Use the second equation if you are older than 60 years

Determine activity factor

Activity level	Activity factor
Low (sedentary)	1.3
Intermediate (some regular exercise)	1.5
High (regular activity or demanding job)	1.7

Total energy expenditure = basal metabolic rate x activity factor

The figures I used as an example I worked out when I was using this program.

So now, if I take my age and weight 78 Kg and use the WHO formula and put my activity level at 1.5 I will come out at a value of 2674 calories expended to stay at the same weight.

That is not too far from 2620 calories so perhaps that is the value for me to stay at the same weight.

However you do it, using my book's formulas or the World health organizations calculations or trial and error you should arrive at a *same weight energy allowance per day (SWEAD) value for yourself.*

So the big task this week is to try to determine what **your** same weight energy allowance per day is..
If you are having difficulties contact us at **www.beatthebulge.co.za** and tell us about your problem. We will help to find a solution.

Now you have a Target to aim at.

What is yours?

SWEAD Same Weight Energy Allowance per day =

Week 9

Tasks

- Use all your strategies
- Research and document low energy snacks
- Develop a list of usual foods
- Develop a list of "danger foods"
- Display lists in helpful locations

This week you must use all the usual strategies and keep on playing the tape. It is good for keeping the momentum going and good for invoking the relaxation response.

The major tasks are the new additions of finding low energy value snack foods you can use as a stop gap. Instead of that chocolate or that packet of crisps it would be far better for you to have some celery sticks or carrots to eat. Obviously it would be better to have snacks that suit your taste buds and not mine.

Just by putting in the Google search engine the following:-"low calorie value snacks" I was given 140,000 hits and the first hit revealed the following– I put it into a table and converted the calories to Kilojoules:

Snacks	Amount	Calories	Kilojoules
Ginger Snaps (Sunshine)	7 pieces	130	546
Ginger Snaps (Nabisco)	4 pieces	120	504
Vanilla Wafer (Keebler)	8 pieces	130	546
(McDonald's) Soft Serve Ice cream	small	150	630

Hostess Light - Crumb Cake	2 pieces	150	630
Hostess Light - Chocolate Cup Cake	1 piece	120	504
Entenmann's fat free - lemon danish	1/6 ring	130	546
Entenmann's fat free - Coffee cake	1/6 cake	130	546
Entenmann's fat free - golden loaf	1/8 cake	130	546
Pudding Jell-O sugar/fat free	1/2 cup	80	336
Ice Cream Bar - Weight Watcher toffee crunch	1 bar	120	504
Ice Cream Bar - Nestle Crunch reduce fat	1 bar	130	546
Ice Cream (Healthy Choice or Weight Watcher)	1/2 cup	120	504
Sorbet - Haagen Dazs (raspberry)	1/2 cup	120	504
Sorbet - Haagen Dazs (pina colada)	1/2 cup	140	588
Orange Sherbert	1/2 cup	130	546
Animal Crackers (Austins)	15 crackers	130	546

These may not be snacks that you like but this is an example of an easy way to find information. There are also many lower value snacks that you could use.

The best is to make your own table and find out the value of snacks that you enjoy. If you can change your eating pattern to snacking on

174

fruit imagine the health benefits and the weight saving.

E.g. the second "hit' on my search was the Anne Collins site which compared the best and worse snacks

Sweet Snack Foods

Best Calorie Choices

For easier weight loss

TYPE	PORTION	CALORIES	FAT
Cantaloupe Melon	1 small	60	0g
Italian chocolate ice	1 scoop	60	0g
Raisin bread	1 slice	60	1g
Tofutti fudge treat	1 bar	30	0g
Fruit sorbet	1 scoop	60	0g
Fresh mixed fruit	1 cup	50	0g
Creamsicle	1 low-cal	25	0g
Air-popped popcorn	1 cup	30	0g

Worst Calorie Choices

TYPE	PORTION	CALORIES	FAT
Muffin	3oz	410	14g
Candy bar	2oz	300	13g
Almond Croissant	1	420	29g
Buttered popcorn	1 cup	100	5g
Chocolate Chip &	1 cookie	150	7g
Toffee	1 cup	720	0g

So there is a lot of information out there. The important thing is to make it relevant to your own situation.

Put up usual food lists and danger food lists in strategic locations.

This means that you should put up the food values of your usual foods in strategic place as well as your danger or weakness foods. Take the information from previous weeks.

E.g. On the refrigerator

WEAKNESS or DANGER FOODS!!!!!			
Food	Quantity	Cals	Kj
Ice-cream	1 cup	300	1260
Chips/crisps	30g	150	630
French fries	100g	330	1380
Chocolate	30g	155	650
Peanuts	1cup	800	3360
Cream High fat 50%	1Ts	130	546
Cream 35%	1Ts	65	270
Cheese	30g	120	504
RESCUE DAYS			
Rescue day 1		910	3800
Rescue day 2		840	3530

Your own frequently used foods			
Food	Quantity	Cals	Kj
Rice Krispies &Milk	1C & 1C	290	1220
Yoghurt Almarai	125ml	130	550
Coffee milk F/C	1 cup	35	150
Peanut butter sandwich 2 slices bread pb	100 100 20 50	270	1130

Summary of Week 9

Weight at the beginning of the week=

Weight at the end of the week   =

Energy balance
Average of Kilojoules/Cals per day =

Recalculate your SWEAD Same Weight Energy Allowance per Day

        =

Target per day for next week   =

Week 10

Tasks

- Use all your strategies

- Reassess your health at the end of the week

- Plan for the future

Here we are in the last week of your program. Now is the time to refine your help strategies and at the end of the week we want you to re-evaluate your health parameters and make a plan for continuing in the future.

So set your SWEAD— same weight energy assessment for the day,

Use your Tape and adjust it for problem areas you may have

The recordings are now standard but at the end of the week you want to see what you have achieved.

Summary of Week 10

Weight at the beginning of the week =

Weight at the end of the week   =

Energy balance
Average of Kilojoules/Cals per day =

It is at the end of week 10 that you must reevaluate your health?

The parameters below will give you an indication of what you have achieved:

Summary of weight loss for the whole program

Weight at the beginning. Program day 1 =

Weight at the end. Program day 70   =

Comparison of health indicators		
	Start	End
Weight		
Circumference of arm		
Circumference of chest		
Circumference of abdomen		
Circumference of hips		
Blood pressure		
Resting Pulse rate		
Pulse rate after 10 knee bends		
Pulse rate after 20 knee bends		
Fasting Blood Sugar		
Fasting total cholesterol		
Fasting HDL Cholesterol		
Fasting LDL Cholesterol		
Fasting Triglycerides		
Time to PRE of "somewhat hard" exertion		

This should translate into improvements in these aspects of your life.

What do I consider a success?

This program will have been a success if,

1. You have lost weight
2. Your health parameters have improved
3. You now know what it is in your eating pattern puts on the weight and you have developed strategies to improve your health in the future.

Weight loss.
I consider a weight loss of 3 kilogram over this period a success. Anything more is a bonus. If this translates into a sustained weight loss over a year, that should be 12 Kg if you need to lose that amount.
Weight gain usually occurs over a long time span, so achieving weight loss on a permanent basis requires a change in behaviour

Health parameters.
By now you should, in addition to your weight loss, have improved in all your health parameters.

Plan for Life
The most important aspect is now to continue.
You should now have a plan for life and know how to improve your health.

What has happened to you?
The crucial strategy however is to translate the lessons learnt into a permanent lifestyle change.

If it helps to continue using an honesty book you can use the maintenance one or even copy it. Basically all you need is your SWEAD and your Kilocalorie/Kilojoule counter book and to stay with this for your health and your life.

The tasks for the maintenance are as follows:

Maintenance

- Calculate your Same Weight Energy Allowance per Day
- Set Yourself a target for the week
- Use your Hypnosis Tape
- Use your Kilocalorie/Kilojoule counter booklet
- Use all your strategies
- Stay with your program - your life depends upon it!

I trust you have enjoyed the program and that you are now healthier and happier.

Please tell me of your experiences and any suggestions to improve the program will be welcomed.

Please give us feedback at www.beatthebulge.co.za or write to us at
   Beat the Bulge
    328 Burger St
    Pietermaritzburg 3201
     Kwazulu-Natal
     South Africa.

Russel Kirkby.

Acknowledgements:

My wife, Robyn, for her help and support.

My daughter, Julia, who designed the graphics and the cover.

All the patients over the years who have taught me so much.

www.annecollins.com and www.calorieking.com for permission to use their calorie counting facts and figures.

ISBN 141206605-0